YO-AAA-903

GUIDE
TO THE SELECTION
OF MUSICAL INSTRUMENTS
WITH RESPECT TO
PHYSICAL ABILITY AND DISABILITY

developed by the

MOSS REHABILITATION HOSPITAL
SETTLEMENT MUSIC SCHOOL
THERAPEUTIC MUSIC PROGRAM

215- 456-9900

BARBARA ELLIOTT, O.T.R.
Principal Researcher and Author

PAUL MACKS, M.A.
Communications Media

ALLISON DEA, O.T.R., F.A.O.T.A.
THOMAS MATSKO, M.A., C.C.C.
Consultants

BARBARA BENEN
JOHN BROOMALL
JEAN M. BURKS
ROBERT CAPANNA
BERNARD HENDERSON
JANET JAMIESON
JEFFREY KLEIN
GEORGE VILK
Contributing Editors

The research described in this report was sponsored by the Division of Personnel Preparation, Bureau of Education for the Handicapped, Department of Health, Education and Welfare under Project #451AH-70263.

Publication of this Guide was made possible
by a grant from the Barra Foundation Inc.

©1982 by LINC Resources, Inc. All rights reserved. Printed in the United States of America. No part of this publication may be reproduced, stored in a retrieval system, or transmitted, in any form or by means, mechanical, electronic, photocopying, or otherwise without permission. For permission and other rights under this copyright, contact the Settlement Music School, Kardon/Northeast Branch, 3745 Clarendon Avenue, Philadelphia, PA 19114.

"U.S. Copyright is claimed until 1989. Thereafter in the U.S. only, all portions of this work covered by the copyright will be in the public domain. Copyright in other countries remain in effect.

"This work was developed under a contract with the Office of Special Education, Department of Education. The Content, however, does not necessarily reflect the position or policy of OSE/ED and no official endorsement of these materials should be inferred.

"Distribution for this work was arranged by LINC Resources, Inc."

ISBN 0-918812-21-6

Sole Distribution
Magnamusic - Baton
10370 Page Industrial Blvd.
St. Louis, MO 63132

TABLE OF CONTENTS

AUGUSTANA UNIVERSITY COLLEGE
LIBRARY

ACKNOWLEDGEMENTS

We would like to acknowledge with thanks the significant contributions of the following:

the Administration and Professional Staff of the Moss Rehabilitation Hospital, Martin Kaplan, Executive Director and Dr. Bernard Albert, Assistant Director

the faculty and staff of the Settlement Music School, Robert Capanna, Executive Director and Dr. Sol Schoenbach, Executive Director Emeritus

the Boards of Directors of both institutions, and in particular the Therapeutic Music Program Joint Board Committee, Eloise C - C. Sutton, Chairman, Morris Satinsky and Emanuel S. Kardon, Co-Chairmen Emeritus

the Department of Occupational Therapy, College of Allied Health Professions, Temple University

all in Philadelphia, Pennsylvania.

FOREWORD

This GUIDE TO THE SELECTION OF MUSICAL INSTRUMENTS WITH RESPECT TO DISABILITY is designed to aid those who teach the disabled to play musical instruments, for therapy and for pleasure. It grew out of a special Therapeutic Music Program for disabled children developed jointly by the Settlement Music School and Moss Rehabilitation Hospital. As the program evolved, it became clear that there was a surprising gap in our knowledge of what physical abilities are required for the playing of different musical instruments. This Guide was conceived as part of an effort to fill that gap. It presents a fairly complete profile of the basic physiology involved in playing a variety of musical instruments.

The Settlement Music School, a United Way agency and a founding member of the National Guild of Community Schools of the Arts, has been dedicated to community service through music education since its founding in 1908. Ten years ago, the school decided, as part of its mission, to reach out to handicapped children. The school turned to the Moss Rehabilitation Hospital, one of the country's leading private rehabilitation centers, for help. Together the two institutions began to develop an understanding, first, of what a disabled student's potential for the study of musical instruments is; secondly, a method of instrument selection; and, finally, an approach to the special training needs of the disabled.

The Moss Rehabilitation Hospital, also a constituent of the United Way and a member of the Federation of Jewish Agencies, has long been an innovator in the field, particularly in the areas of devising alternative therapies and new services for the disabled. Thus, the hospital was receptive to the suggestion by the Settlement Music School that they create a program to teach the handicapped to play a musical instrument. The hospital felt that, as therapy, instrumental musical study presented many advantages: 1. It involves a wide range of physical activities. There are many different instruments and each instrument demands a specific physical movement. The instrument can be matched to the disability. 2. Learning to play an instrument is, by its nature, geared to a series of graduated goals. 3. The therapy can be carried out in the home as the student practices on the instrument. 4. Compared to other therapies, music study is relatively inexpensive. 5. It also can be very pleasurable.

The result has been a unique collaboration in which hospital and school have united to reach a common goal: to provide specially designed programs of instrumental music study to the disabled in a medically informed and controlled framework. The Therapeutic Music Program is the result of this joint effort. In 1982, over three hundred youths studied in the program, which was offered at various locations throughout the metropolitan Philadelphia area.

The program works in this way. The potential participant is interviewed at the music school and, at the same time, the child's parents are told all about the program, its purpose and procedures. Next, a pediatrician at Moss examines the child to determine if he or she would benefit from the program. If the answer is yes, the doctor formally prescribes the program for the child. At this point, an occupational therapist evaluates the child's physical abilities—vision and perception, status of the child's upper and lower extremities, head/trunk control—and the child's general capacity to perform the activities of daily life. Long term and short term therapeutic goals are determined on the basis of this evaluation. The child's needs and abilities are then compared with the descriptive profile of the physical requirements for playing various instruments listed in this Guide. A list of possible instruments is drawn up, in order from most therapeutic to least helpful. Indications are also given of instruments whose study would be neutral—that is, neither helpful nor harmful—and of instruments whose effect would be deleterious on that particular student. At this point, the selection of an instrument is made, taking into account the child's interest, as well as the professional recommendations of the therapist.

During the course of study, the child works both with specially trained music instructors and with members of the therapeutic staff. The program is structured to encourage close contact between the two staffs, and to insure that frequent checks on the child's progress are made. These periodic reassessments are used to refine and adjust the therapeutic and musical goals set for the child and lead ultimately to a successful outcome for the child.

Although the Guide was specifically developed for use in our Therapeutic Music Program, we believe it to have wide application as an aid to instrument selection for the physically handicapped. It is designed to give professionals involved in providing therapy for the handicapped through the study of musical instruments a common ground of understanding, and a point of departure for reaching a detailed individual assessment of the needs and abilities of disabled persons.

INTRODUCTION

This Guide is specifically designed to assist the music teacher and therapist in the selection of an appropriate instrument for students with physical handicaps. Much of the data presented relates directly to the act of playing and forms the primary basis for making a judgment as to the suitability of a particular instrument for a particular child. Other data relates to collateral requirements such as tuning or transportation of the instrument which should not be used as determining criteria, but are presented so that potentially frustrating situations may be anticipated and avoided.

The Guide is organized according to instrumental families: Strings, Woodwinds, Brass, Percussion and Keyboard. There is an introduction to each family, which lists all instruments in the group and provides basic information as to how they produce and alter sound. An Instrument Selection Guide follows that lists in easily accessible tabular form the various instruments in the group and the specific physical limitations that might affect the playing of each instrument. Individual instruments in the group are then discussed in detail, according to the following outline.

I. *General Information and Descriptive Data*
   Photographs depict overall body position, specific prehension patterns and instrument details. The musicians were directed to pose in positions which would indicate both normal and extreme playing positions.
   Section Heading includes instrument family, name and type; make and model examined; and materials used in the construction of the instrument. The specific make and model chosen does not constitute an endorsement of these instruments over any other. Selection was based on availability, the experience of music instructors consulted, and an attempt to consider those instruments most commonly used by students.

II. *Information on Secondary Requirements*
   Assembly section described procedures necessary for cleaning and transport of the instruments.
   Tuning Requirements describe the physical manipulation needed to prepare the instrument for play.
   Transport section gives information as to the dimensions of the instrument case, weight of the instrument with case; and presence of handles, latches, or special retaining devices inside the case are noted where significant.
   Student Maintenance describes routine tuning, cleaning, or replacement of perishable components that may be anticipated throughout the course of study.
   Variations among Manufacturers describes significant differences between comparable instruments (although not all minor deviations are noted since there are many).
   Other Devices lists auxiliary equipment where applicable.

III. *Checklist*
   This checklist indicating specific needs for each instrument may be used to compare a student's ability for functional independence on various instruments selected as appropriate.

IV. *Analysis of Physical Requirements*
   This section includes a general description of the physical requirements for playing the instrument, including: general body position and major body parts involved; major muscle groups and movement observed; muscle strength and speed and dexterity; sensation and perception; respiration and cardiac output; and vision and audition.

This data, in conjunction with the "Major Muscle Groups Used in Playing" chart and the "Movement Observed in Playing" chart which follow, is the primary data on which an occupational therapist would base instrument selection. This information constitutes a descriptive model of the physical requirement for play, and should be used both as an assessment of the student's current capabilities and a description of possible therapies available through instrumental study.

While the Guide touches on most basic information pertaining to the nuts and bolts of music study for the disabled child, it is important to note that the services of skilled and sympathetic music instructors and occupational therapists are vital, as well as the maximum involvement of the parents and child. While we attempt to include most of the information needed for an intelligent choice of instruments, the most important component, the child's own desire and dream to study a particular instrument cannot of course be included. Our experience suggests that this desire, properly channelled and intelligently guided, is the true key to a successful musical, and therapeutic, experience.

FAMILY: STRINGS

INSTRUMENTS: VIOLIN

                 VIOLA

                 CELLO (Violoncello)

                 STRING BASS (Upright)

                 ELECTRIC GUITAR

                 ACOUSTIC GUITAR

                 ELECTRIC BASS GUITAR

INTRODUCTION

The violin, viola, cello, and bass produce sound by vibrations that result from the bow being drawn across the strings, or by plucking. Plucking (or "pizzicato") is often the rule for an upright (acoustic) bass when playing certain types of music; it is the exception for the violin, viola, and cello.

Depressing a string until it contacts the fingerboard beneath it alters its vibrating length and thus causes a change in sounding pitch. The body of the instrument serves as a resonating chamber, which amplifies the strings' sound and colors their tone. The point at which a tuned string should be depressed to produce a given pitch is unmarked on these instruments.

The acoustic guitar, electric guitar, and electric bass are fretted instruments, e.g., the point at which a tuned string should be depressed in order to produce a given pitch is marked by frets, raised metal bands that run across the width of the instrument's neck. A string is depressed until it comes into solid contact with one of the frets and this adjusts its sounding length. Picks may be used on the guitars to pluck an individual string or cause several or all of the strings to sound simultaneously.

INSTRUMENT SELECTION GUIDE

An "X" indicates a potential physical limitation in relationship to "normal" use of the instrument. The presence of an "X" should not necessarily preclude consideration of the instrument if compensatory techniques and adaptations are appropriate.

Potential Limitations	Violin	Viola	Cello	Bass	Accoust. Guitar	Elec. Guitar	Bass Guitar
Contractures of							
Neck		X					
Shoulders	X	X	X	X	X	X	X
Elbows	X	X	X	X	X	X	X
Wrists	X	X	X	X	X	X	X
Fingers	X	X	X	X	X	X	X
Hips			X	X			
Knees				X			
Ankles				X			
Incoordination							
Gross – Upper Extremities	X	X	X	X			X
– Lower Extremities							
Fine – Upper Extremities	X	X	X	X	X	X	X
– Lower Extremities							
Limb Loss (prosthesis fit implied)							
– Upper Extremities							
– Above Elbow	X	X	X	X	X	X	X
– Below Elbow	X	X	X	X	X	X	X
– Partial Hand	X	X	X	X	X	X	X
–Lower Extremities							
– Below Knee			X	X			
– Above Knee			X	X			
– Symes				X			

Potential Limitations	Violin	Viola	Cello	Bass	Accoust. Guitar	Elec. Guitar	Bass Guitar
Spasticity – Upper Extremities	X	X	X	X	X	X	X
– Lower Extremities			X				
Weakness							
Proximal – Head/Neck	X	X					
Shoulder	X	X	X	X	X	X	X
Trunk	X	X	X	X	X	X	X
Distal – Upper Extremities	X	X	X	X	X	X	X
– Lower Extremities				X			

Violin in normal playing position

Comparison of Half (left) and Full size Violin

Left hand position in extreme (upper register) play of Violin

Right, Bow hand position in play of Violin

FAMILY: Strings
INSTRUMENT: Violin

TYPE (SIZES):	1/16	1/8	1/4	1/2	3/4	4/4 (Full)
MAKE:	Suzuki	Suzuki	Suzuki	Suzuki	Framus	Skylark
MODEL:	Kiso	Nagoya	Nagoya	Nagoya	Not Indicated	Not Indicated

MATERIALS USED IN CONSTRUCTION: Wood

I. Assembly and Disassembly

The violin and bow are not disassembled by the student although physical manipulation, such as loosening of bow tension, may be required. See *Tuning Requirements* and *Student Maintenance*.

II. Tuning Requirements

Strings are tuned by twisting the wooden peg located at the scroll end of the instrument. Pegs are tapered for friction fit. Pegs are turned using thumb and second finger of left hand in clockwise or counterclockwise direction against some resistance. Pressure must also be directed toward the peg retaining hole in order to prevent slippage when the desired string tension is reached. This results in a combination turning and pushing movement. This process is accomplished with the instrument maintained in playing position between the chin and shoulder. The left hand is used to manipulate pegs on both sides of the scroll while the bow is drawn across the strings with the right hand in order to test for accuracy of intonation.

Instruments are also provided with fine tuning devices. The fine tuners are small clamp-like metal constructions that are attached to the strings of the instrument between the bridge and tailpiece. The turning of a small screw with a head diameter of 6 mm (.23 inches) and serrated edges increases or diminishes the amount of tension on the string.

III. Transport

All instruments are provided with a hard shell (wood composition) case which serves as a protective container and assists transport.

All cases have one handle and two latches.

The instrument is laid in its case for transport; however, the bow is retained in the lid. One end of the bow is slid into a pocket and the other end is supported by a rectangular spring. The spring is drawn away from the lid at one end and the bow slips through the opening created. Some cases examined were different in that the retainer did not form a rectangle but remained open on one side. The bow is pushed through the existing opening and held by tension.

IV. Student Maintenance

A. Tuning
The instrument must be tuned both before and during play.
B. Bow Tension
Bow tension may also need to be adjusted during play. This is accomplished by turning an octagonal bolt head 7 to 9 mm (.28 to .35 inches) in diameter and 14 to 18 mm (.55 to .71 inches) long located at the end of the bow above the frog. The bolt head is gripped between the thumb and second finger and turned in a clockwise or counterclockwise direction against some resistance. Both hands are needed for this operation.
C. Cleaning
The body of the instrument must be cleaned and polished with a soft cloth.
D. Rosining
In order to maintain the necessary friction between both hair and strings, rosin is ap-

plied to the bow. This may be necessary during play and involves the passing of a small bar 60 mm x 30 mm x 20 mm (2.36 x 1.18 x .79 inches) over the hairs. Two hands are needed for this operation.

E. Replacement of strings

Strings deteriorate with age and break. They may also break owing to overtensioning during the tuning process.

Strings on the instruments examined are known as "ball end" strings. The ball is actually a metal ring which prevents the string from slipping through its opening in the tailpiece. Replacing a string involves threading the plain end through a hole in the tailpiece, routing it over the bridge and nut, and then threading it through another hole located in the tuning peg. The peg is then used to wind up excessive string length (in some instances the string must be cut beforehand). The instrument is then tuned.

V. Variation Among Manufacturers

A. Instruments

Instruments may vary slightly in outside dimensions, depending upon the maker.

Variations within a given size are not considered significant.

B. Bows

Bows may vary in overall length by as much as 25 mm (.98 inches), but this will not necessarily affect the overall weight or playing length.

C. Strings

Strings are manufactured from several different materials. Choice is a matter of musical preference rather than physical requirements. Strings are manufactured with plain ends or looped ends. A plain-ended string must be threaded through its opening in the tailpiece and is then retained by tying a special knot. This type of string is at least as common as the ball type. Strings with looped ends are connected directly to a fine tuner.

D. Chin Rests

Various types of chin rests are available and may assist the student in supporting the instrument. If a chin rest other than that supplied with the instrument is used, it may require additional assembly and disassembly in order to fit the instrument into its case.

E. Shoulder Pads

Violins are often provided with a pad that is attached to the bottom of the instrument. These devices may assist the student in supporting the instrument. The addition of any such device, while it may be desirable, could require additional assembly and disassembly in order to fit the instrument into its case.

Checklist

The following skills are necessary for independence in playing, owning, and receiving instruction on this instrument. The music teacher should confirm the need for those items, such as need for transport, which may not be necessary in all situations. The teacher should also add any items, such as the need to transport instructional materials to and from lessons, which may be applicable.

The therapist should indicate those requirements which a student is able to fulfill. The teacher or parents must provide for assistance in those areas in which a student may be dependent.

	Needed	Can Perform	Can Not Perform
1. Tune Instrument	_____	_____	_____
2. Transport instrument	_____	_____	_____
3. Place instrument in case	_____	_____	_____
4. Open and close case	_____	_____	_____
5. Clean instrument	_____	_____	_____
6. Replace broken strings	_____	_____	_____
7. Place instrument in playing position	_____	_____	_____
8. Rosin bow	_____	_____	_____
9. Adjust bow hair tension	_____	_____	_____
10. Adjust or install chin rest	_____	_____	_____
11. Adjust or install shoulder rest.	_____	_____	_____

A Full-sized violin was analyzed. The 1/2 and 3/4-sized violins, when fitted to individual needs, utilize the same components as the full size.

Considerations:
- General Body Position
- Major Body Parts Involved in Playing - Mobile/Stable Components - Functions of Major/Minor Joints Involved - Mobile/ Stable Capacity

The violin is played in a manner requiring support (*stability*) and movement (*mobility*) of head/neck, trunk, and upper extremities. The major individual joints that are required to function in a stable capacity are the neck, left shoulder, and right hand. Movement is of major importance in joints of the right shoulder, both elbows, wrists, and left fingers.

Considerations:
- Major Muscle Groups
- Movement Observed

The violin utilizes muscle groups to produce stabilization, flexion, abduction, adduction, rotation, and pronation/supination of both upper extremities. Wrist and hand movements include flexion, extension, and deviation. The degree of movement is greater for the right shoulder and left wrist and fingers. Movement is used to a lesser degree in elbows and right wrist.

Considerations: • Muscle Strength
                 • Speed/Dexterity

Muscle strength utilized bilaterally in playing the violin requires holding the instrument up against gravity (Fair+ muscle grade) for periods of time. Additional strength is required of left hand to depress string or strings (Good- to Good muscle grade) increasing with playing time. Changes of height of strings from fingerboard can increase or decrease resistance. The weight of bow increases strength requirement of right hand slightly, with more strength demanded when force is applied in bowing against gravity (Good- to Good muscle grade). The speed/dexterity of left hand for fingering relies on rapid alternating up/down movements with individual, coupled, and mass digit execution.

Considerations: • Sensation
                 • Perception

Playing the violin appears to utilize the deep sensations for arm movements and depressing strings with tactile discrimination for finger placement. Perceptual components appear to be in the areas of orientation, visual and motor. (Exclude visual for non-sighted individuals.) Orientation mechanisms direct body movements using visual cues in a planned coordinated manner.

Considerations: • Respiration
                 • Cardiac Output

The playing of the violin requires moderate exertion (light work) which may increase with prolonged playing. Respiration must be adequate to maintain level of exertion without signs of fatigue.

Considerations: • Vision
                 • Audition

The violin may be played by sighted individuals and also by those at any level of visual impairment. (Tactile/kinesthetic modalities may be primarily relied upon.) Auditory levels most functional are in the normal to moderate impairment range.

VIOLIN

MAJOR MUSCLE GROUPS USED IN PLAYING
WITHOUT SUBSTITUTION OR ADAPTATION

KEY: B=Beginning Level   P=Held Position for Playing
            I=Intermediate Level   X=Muscle Movement Used in Playing
            A=Advanced Level   •=Increased Usage

Body Part	Function	Muscle or Muscle Groups	Left B	Left I	Left A	Right B	Right I	Right A
Neck	Flexion & Rotation	Sternocleidomastoideus	x	•	•	x		
Scapula	Stabilization	Serratus (Anterior)						
	Abduction	Trapezius (Superior)						
	Elevation	Trapezius (Inferior)	x					
	Depression	Trapezius (Middle)						
	Adduction	Rhomboideus Major & Minor						
Shoulder	Flexion	Deltoideus (Anterior)	p			x		
	Abduction	Deltoideus (Middle)	x			x	•	•
	Horizontal Adduction	Pectoralis Major	p					
	External Rotation	External Rotator Group	x	•	•			
	Internal Rotation	Internal Rotator Group	x	•	•			
Elbow	Flexion	Biceps Brachii	x			x		
		Brachialis						
Forearm	Supination	Supinator Group	x			p		
Wrist	Deviation, Radial	Flexor Carpi Radial.	x			x		
		Extensor Carpi Rad. Longus						
	Deviation, Ulnar	Flexor Carpi Ulnaris		•	•			
	Extension	Extensor Carpi Ulnaris	x			x		
		Extensor Carpi Ulnaris	x			x		

Body Part	Function	Muscle or Muscle Groups	Left B	I	A	Right B	I	A
	Flexion	Flexor Carpi Radial.						
		Flexor Carpi Ulnaris	x			x		
Fingers	MP Flexion	Lumbricales	x			p		
	IP Flexion (1st)	Flex. Digit. Superior	x			p		
	IP Flexion (2nd)	Flex. Digit. Prof.	x			p		
	MP Extension	Ext. Digit. Com.	x					
	Adduction	Interossei Palmares	x			p		
	Abduction	Interossei Dorsales	x	•	•			
	Abduction	Abduct. Digit. Min.	x	•	•			
Thumb	Abduction	Abduct. Poll. Longus	p			p		

Muscles listed are used in the playing of this instrument; those not listed are not directly involved.

Facial and neck musculature is marked on right and left for convenience.
Increases (•) are noted in Intermediate Level and Advanced Level that are most obvious.
Muscles are used in groups for synergist movements rather than as isolated muscle movements.
Generally X's in Beginning Level continue in Intermediate and Advanced Levels.

VIOLIN

MOVEMENT OBSERVED IN PLAYING
(ACTIVE & POSITIONAL)
WITHOUT SUBSTITUTION OR ADAPTATION*

These ranges were determined through working with musicians. They reflect the musician's body size, individuality, and possibly style. The ranges are approximate to give a working baseline for instrument suitability.

Head:		Lateral flexion (20°) is used to hold instrument under chin.
Shoulders:	Left	Flexed (40°), internal rotation (60°), adducted (-40°) across chest.
	Right	Flexes (60 to -20°) with abduction (0 - 60°) and internal rotation (45°).
Elbows:	Left	Flexes (70° - 100°). Adduction, external rotation increase as flexion increases.
	Right	Flexes (10 - 90°) with shoulder abducted and internally rotated.
Forearms:	Left	Full range of supination utilized.
	Right	Held in full range of pronation.
Wrists:	Left	Flexes full range as fingers advance to bridge and extends (0 - 30°) at scroll end. Radial deviation is complete during play.
	Right	Extended (30°) with (5 - 10°) ulnar and radial deviation included at tip and tail of bow.
Thumbs:	Left	Stabilizes fingers around neck at (70°) abduction.
	Right	Held in abduction under index finger on bow as in functional resting fashion.
Fingers:	Left	All fingers use full range of MP flexion, PIP flexion, DIP flexion, abduction and adduction during play.
	Right	Fingers held in functional resting position with bow placed horizontal to palm (45°) MP flexion, (30°) PIP flexion, (20°) DIP flexion.

*I.e., using normal body position for playing, without any devices for instrument or body parts.

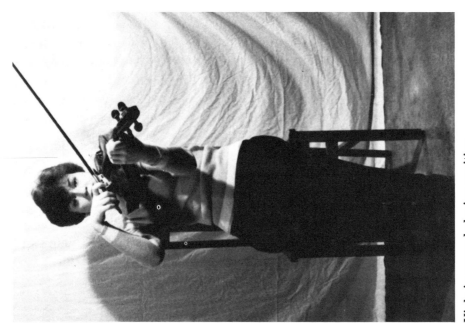

**Viola in normal playing position,
Bow "at the frog" (Beginning of Down Bow)**

**Viola in normal playing position,
Bow "at the point" (Beginning of up Bow)**

16

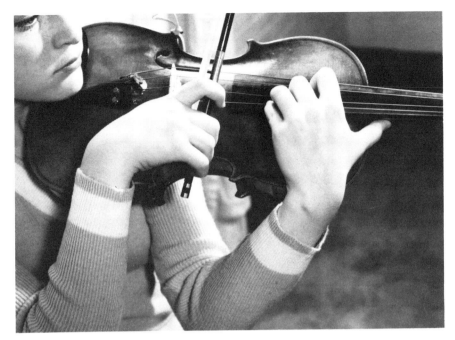

Left hand position in extreme (upper register) play of Viola

Left hand position in normal (low-middle register) play of Viola

FAMILY: Strings
INSTRUMENT: Viola
SIZE: Full (15-1/2" Body)
MAKE: Hoffner
MATERIALS USED IN CONSTRUCTION: Wood

I. Assembly and Disassembly
The viola and bow are not disassembled by the student although physical manipulation, such as loosening of the bow tension, may be required. See *Tuning Requirements*
and *Student Maintenance.*

II. Tuning Requirements
Strings are tuned by twisting the wooden pegs located at the scroll end of the instrument. Pegs are tapered for friction fit. Pegs are turned using thumb and second finger
of left hand in clockwise or counterclockwise direction against some resistance.
Pressure must also be directed toward the peg retaining hole in order to prevent slippage when the desired string tension is reached. This results in a combination turning
and pushing movement. This process is accomplished with the instrument maintained in playing position between the chin and shoulder. The left hand is used to
manipulate pegs on both sides of the scroll while the bow is drawn across the strings
with the right hand in order to test for accuracy of intonation.

Instruments are also provided with fine tuning devices. The fine tuners are small
clamp-like metal constructions that are attached to the strings of the instrument between the bridge and .39 inch tailpiece. The turning of a small screw with a head
diameter of 10 mm and serrated edges increases or diminishes the amount of tension
on the string.

III. Transport
All instruments are provided with a hard shell (plastic composition) case which serves
as a protective container and assists transport.

The instrument is laid in its case for transport; however the bow is retained in the lid.
One end of the bow is slid into a pocket and the other end is supported by a rectangular spring. The spring is drawn away from the lid at one end and bow slips
through the opening created.

IV. Student Maintenance
A. Tuning
The instrument must be tuned both before and during play.
B. Bow Tension
Bow tension may also need to be adjusted during play. This is accomplished by turn-
ing an octagonal bolt head 8.0 mm (.31 inch) in diameter and 15 mm (.59 inch) in
length located at the end of the bow above the frog. The bolt head is gripped between
the thumb and second finger and turned in a clockwise or counterclockwise direction
against some resistance. Both hands are needed for this operation.
C. Cleaning
The body of the instrument must be cleaned and polished with a soft cloth.
D. Rosining
In order to maintain the necessary friction between bow hair and strings, rosin is applied to the bow. This may be necessary during play and involves the passing of a
small bar 60 mm x 30 x 20 mm (2.36 x 1.18 x .79 inches) over the hairs. Two hands are
needed for this operation.
E. Replacement of Strings
Strings deteriorate with age and break. They may also break owing to overtensioning
during the tuning process. Strings on the instrument examined are known as "ball

end" strings. The ball is actually a metal ring which prevents the string from slipping through its opening in the tailpiece. Replacing a string involves threading the plain end through a hole in the tailpiece, routing it over the bridge and nut, and then threading it through another hole located in the tuning peg. The peg is then used to wind up excessive string length (in some instances the string must be cut beforehand). The instrument is then tuned.

V. Variation Among Manufacturers
   A. Instruments
   Instruments may vary slightly in outside dimensions, depending upon the maker. Variation within a given size is not considered significant.
   B. Bows
   Bows may vary in overall length by as much as 25 mm but this will not necessarily affect the overall weight or playing length.
   C. Strings
   Strings are manufactured from several different materials; choice is a matter of musical preference rather than physical requirements. Strings are also manufactured with plain ends and looped ends. A plain-ended string must be threaded through its opening in the tailpiece and is then retained by tying a special knot. This type of string is at least as common as the ball type. Strings with looped ends are connected directly to a fine tuner.
   D. Chin Rests
   Various types of chin rests are available and may assist the student in supporting the instrument. If a chin rest other than that supplied with the instrument is used, it may require additional assembly and disassembly in order to fit the instrument into its case.
   E. Shoulder Pads
   Violas are often provided with a pad that is attached to the bottom of the instrument. These devices may assist the student in supporting the instrument. The addition of any such device, while it may be desirable, may require additional assembly and disassembly in order to fit the instrument into its case.

Checklist

The following skills are necessary for independence in playing, owning, and receiving instruction on this instrument. The music teacher should confirm the need for those items, such as need for transport, which may not be necessary in all situations. The teacher should also add any items, such as the need to transport instructional materials to and from lessons, which may be applicable.

The therapist should indicate those requirements which a student is able to fulfill. The teacher or parents must provide for assistance in those areas in which a student may be dependent.

	Needed	Can Perform	Can Not Perform
1. Tune instrument			
2. Transport instrument			
3. Place instrument in case			
4. Open and close case			
5. Clean instrument			
6. Replace broken strings			
7. Place instrument in playing position			
8. Rosin bow			
9. Adjust bow hair tension			
10. Adjust or install chin rest			
11. Adjust or install shoulder rest			

VIOLA

A full-sized viola was analyzed. The 1/2 and 3/4 violas, when fitted to individual needs, utilize the same components as the full size.

Considerations:
- General Body Position
- Major Body parts Involved in Playing - Mobile/Stable Components - Functions of Major/Minor Joints Involved - Mobile/Stable capacity.

The viola is played in a manner requiring support (*stability*) and movement (*mobility*) of head/neck, trunk, and upper extremities. The major individual joints that are required to function in a stable capacity are those of the left shoulder, right wrist, right hand, and thumb of left hand. Movement is of major importance in joints of right shoulder, both elbows, left wrist, and fingers of left hand.

Considerations:
- Major Muscle Groups
- Movement Observed

The viola utilizes muscle groups to produce stability, rotation, flexion, and abduction of the upper extremities. Wrist and hand movements include pronation, supination, flexion, extension, abduction, and adduction. The degree of movement is greatest for right shoulder, right elbow, and fingers of the left hand. Movement is used to a lesser degree in left elbow and left wrist.

Considerations:
- Muscle Strength
- Speed/Dexterity

Muscle strength utilized in playing the viola requires holding the instrument up against gravity (Fair+ muscle grade) for periods of time. Additional strength is required of the left hand to depress string or strings increasing with playing time (Good- to Good muscle grade). Changes in height of strings from fingerboard can increase or decrease resistance. The weight of the bow in the right hand increases strength requirement slightly except when downward force against strings is required (Good muscle grade).

The speed and dexterity of the left hand for fingering relies on rapid alternating, up and down, and sliding movements with individual coupled and mass digit execution, increasing with advanced playing.

Considerations:
- Sensation
- Perception

Playing the viola appears to utilize the deep sensations for arm and hand movements and depressing strings requires tactile discrimination for finger placement. Perceptual components appear to be in the areas of orientation, visual and motor. (Exclude visual for non-sighted individuals.) Orientation directs body movement, using visual cues and in a planned, coordinated manner.

Considerations:
- Respiration
- Cardiac Output

Playing of the viola requires moderate exertion (light work), which may increase with prolonged playing. Respiration must be adequate to maintain level of exertion without signs of fatigue.

Considerations:
- Vision
- Audition

The viola may be played by sighted individuals and also by those at any level of visual impairment. (Tactile/kinesthetic modalities may be primarily relied upon.) Auditory levels most functional are in the normal to moderate impairment range.

VIOLA

MAJOR MUSCLE GROUPS USED IN PLAYING
WITHOUT SUBSTITUTION OR ADAPTATION

KEY:
B = Beginning Level
I = Intermediate Level
A = Advanced Level

P = Held Position for Playing
X = Muscle Movement Used in Playing
• = Increased Usage

Body Part	Function	Muscle or Muscle Groups	Left B	Left I	Left A	Right B	Right I	Right A
Neck	Flexion & Rotation	Sternocleidomastoideus	p	—	—	p	—	—
Scapula	Stabilization	Serratus (Anterior)	p	—	—	p	—	—
	Abduction	Trapezius (Superior)						
	Elevation	Trapezius (Inferior)						
	Depression	Trapezius (Middle)						
	Adduction	Rhomboideus Major & Minor						
Shoulder	Flexion	Deltoideus (Anterior)	p	—	—	p	—	—
	Abduction	Deltoideus (Middle)	x	—	—	x	—	—
	Horizontal Adduction	Pectoralis Major	x	•	•	—	—	—
	External Rotation	External Rotator Group	x	•	•	—	—	—
	Internal Rotation	Internal Rotator Group	—	—	—	x	•	•
Elbow	Flexion	Biceps Brachii Brachialis	x	•	•	x	—	—
Forearm	Supination	Supinator Group	x	—	—	—	—	—
	Pronation	Pronator Group	x	—	—	p	—	—
Wrist	Deviation, Radial	Flexor Carpi Radial. / Extensor Carpi Rad. Longus / Extensor Carpi Rad. Brevis	x	—	—	x	—	—
	Deviation, Ulnar	Flexor Carpi Ulnaris						

Body Part	Function	Muscle or Muscle Groups	Left B	Left I	Left A	Right B	Right I	Right A
	Extension	Extensor Carpi Ulnaris	x	—	—	x	—	—
		Extensor Carpi Rad. Longus & Brevis		—	—		—	—
		Extensor Carpi Ulnaris	x	—	—	x	—	—
	Flexion	Flexor Carpi Radial.	x	—	—	x	—	—
		Flexor Carpi Ulnaris	x	—	—	x	—	—
Fingers	MP Flexion	Lumbricales	x	—	—	p	—	—
	IP Flexion (1st)	Flex. Digit. Superior	x	—	—	p	—	—
	IP Flexion (2nd)	Flex. Digit. Prof.	x	—	—	p	—	—
	MP Extension	Ext. Digit. Com.	x	—	—		—	—
	Adduction	Interossei Palmares	x	—	—		—	—
	Abduction	Interossei Dorsales	x	•	•	p	—	—
		Abduct. Digit. Min.	x	—	—	p	—	—
Thumb	Abduction	Abduct. Poll. Brevis		—	—		—	—
		Abduct. Poll. Longus	p	—	—	p	—	—

Muscles listed are used in the playing of this instrument; those not listed are not directly involved.

Facial and neck musculature is marked on right and left for convenience.
Increases (•) are noted in Intermediate Level and Advanced Level that are most obvious.
Muscles are used in groups for synergist movements rather than as isolated muscle movements.
Generally X's in Beginning Level continue in Intermediate and Advanced Levels.

VIOLA

MOVEMENT OBSERVED IN PLAYING
(ACTIVE & POSITIONAL)
WITHOUT SUBSTITUTION OR ADAPTATION*

These ranges were determined through working with musicians. They reflect the musician's body size, individuality, and possibly style. The ranges are approximate to give a working baseline for instrument suitability.

Head:		Lateral flexion (20°) is used to hold instrument under chin.
Shoulders:	Left	Flexed (40°) with external rotation (60°) and adducted (-30°) across chest.
	Right	Flexes (40-60°) with abduction (20-90°) and internal rotation (45°).
Elbows:	Left	Flexes (40-90°). Adduction and external rotation increase as flexion increases.
	Right	Flexes (20-90°) with shoulder abduction and internal rotation.
Forearms:	Left	Full range of supination used during play.
	Right	Held in full pronated position for bowing.
Wrists:	Left	Flexes (0-30°) with full range of ulnar deviation as fingers advance to bridge.
	Right	Extends (0-30°) with ulnar deviation (0-30°) used when tip of bow is used.
Thumbs:	Left	Stabilizes fingers around neck at (60°) abduction.
	Right	Held in abduction under finger on bow as in a functional resting position.
Fingers:	Left	All fingers use full range of MP flexion, PIP flexion, DIP flexion, abduction and adduction during play.
	Right	Fingers held in flexed, functional resting fashion with bow placed horizontal to palm, MP (30°), PIP (30°), DIP (20°).

*i.e., using normal body position for playing, without any devices for instrument or body parts.

Cello in normal playing position

Right, Bow hand position in play of Cello

Left hand position in extreme (upper register) play of Cello

Left hand position in normal (low-middle register) play of Cello

FAMILY: Strings
INSTRUMENT: Cello (Violoncello)
SIZE: Full Size
MAKE: Englehardt   3/4 Roth
MODEL: E55   50C
MATERIALS USED IN CONSTRUCTION: Wood

Note: Both sizes examined are readily available as standard items of manufacture. Selection of appropriate size for instruction is a decision that must be made by a teacher familiar with the sizing requirements of the individual student.

I.   Assembly and Disassembly
     The cello and bow are not disassembled by the student although physical manipulation, such as loosening of bow tension, may be required. See *Tuning Requirements* and *Student Maintenance.*

II. Tuning Requirements
     Strings are tuned by twisting the wooden pegs located at the scroll end of the instrument. Pegs are tapered for friction fit. Pegs are turned using thumb and second finger of left hand in a clockwise or counterclockwise direction against some resistance. Pressure may also need to be directed toward the peg retaining hole in order to prevent slippage when the desired string tension is reached. This results in a combination turning and pushing movement. This process is usually accomplished with the instrument in playing position between the legs. The left hand is used to manipulate pegs on both sides of the scroll while the bow is drawn across the strings with the right hand in order to test for accuracy of intonation.

     Most instruments are also provided with fine-tuning devices. The fine tuners are small clamp-like metal structures that are attached to the tailpiece of the instrument behind the bridge. The turning of a small screw with a head diameter of 12 mm (.47 inches) and serrated edges increases or decreases the amount of tension on the string.

III. Transport
     The instruments are provided with a canvas bag that serves as a protective container and assists transport. The bag is opened along its length through the use of a heavy zipper. A cloth handle is provided near where the body of the instrument slopes toward the neck. The bow is slipped into its own compartment, which is secured by a snap. Weight and dimensional increases are negligible.

IV. Student Maintenance
     A. Tuning
        The instrument must be tuned both before and during play.
     B. Bow Tension
        Bow tension may also need to be adjusted during play. This is accomplished by turning an octagonal bolt head 9.0 mm (.35 inches) in diameter and 17 mm (.67 inches) long located at the end of the bow above the frog. The bolt head is gripped between the thumb and second finger and turned in a clockwise or counterclockwise direction against some resistance. Both hands are needed for this operation.
     C. Cleaning
        The body of the instrument must be cleaned and polished with a soft cloth.
     D. Rosining
        In order to maintain the necessary friction between bow hair and strings, rosin is applied to the bow. This may be necessary during play and involves the passing of a small bar 60 mm x 30 mm x 20 mm (2.36 x 1.18 x .79 inches) over the hairs. Two hands are needed for this operation.

E. Replacement of Strings
   Strings deteriorate with age and break. They may also break owing to overtensioning during the tuning process. Strings on the instrument examined are known as "ball

   end" strings. The ball is actually a metal ring which prevents the string from slipping through its opening in the tailpiece. Replacing a string involves threading the plain end through a hole in the tailpiece, routing it over the bridge and nut, and then threading it through another hole in the tuning peg. The peg is then used to wind up excessive string length (in some instances the string must be cut beforehand). The instrument is then tuned.

V. Variation Among Manufacturers
   A. Instruments
      Instruments may vary slightly 15 mm (.59 inches) in outside dimensions, depending upon the maker. Variation within a given size is not considered significant.
   B. Bows
      Bows may vary in overall length by as much as 25 mm (.98 inches), but this will not necessarily affect the overall weight or playing length.
   C. Strings
      Strings are manufactured from several different materials. Choice is a matter of musical preference rather than physical requirements. Strings are also manufactured with plain ends or looped ends. A plain-ended string must be threaded through its opening in the tailpiece and is then retained by tying a special knot. This type of string is at least as common as the ball type. Strings with looped ends are connected directly to a fine tuner.
   D. Cases
      Hard shell cases are available for the cello. Outside dimensions may increase by 100 mm (3.94 inches). Weight of instrument with case may exceed 9.8 kg (21.61 lb.).
   E. Endpin
      The endpins on some instruments may be angled to assist support. These pins are not retractable and must be removed for transport.

Checklist

The following skills are necessary for independence in playing, owning, and receiving instruction on this instrument. The music teacher should confirm the need for those items, such as need for transport, which may not be necessary in all situations. The teacher should also add any items, such as the need to transport instructional materials to and from lessons, which may be applicable.

The therapist should indicate those requirements which a student is able to fulfill. The teacher or parents must provide for assistance in those areas in which a student may be dependent.

	Needed	Can Perform	Can Not Perform
1. Tune instrument	————	——————	————
2. Transport instrument	————	——————	————
3. Place instrument in case	————	——————	————
4. Open and close case	————	——————	————
5. Clean instrument	————	——————	————
6. Replace broken strings	————	——————	————
7. Place instrument in playing position	————	——————	————
8. Rosin bow	————	——————	————
9. Adjust bow tension	————	——————	————
10. Adjust endpin	————	——————	————

CELLO

A full-sized cello was analyzed. The 1/2 and 3/4 cellos, when fitted to individual needs, utilize the same components as the full size.

Considerations:
- General Body Position
- Major Body Parts Involved in Playing - Mobile/Stable Components - Functions of Major/Minor Joints Involved - Mobile/ Stable Capacity.

The cello is played in a manner requiring support (stability) and movement (mobility) of trunk, upper extremities, and lower extremities. The major individual joints that are required to function in a stable capacity are those of the right wrist and right hand.. Movement is of major importance in joints of the shoulders, elbows, left wrist, and left hand.

Considerations:
- Major Muscle Groups
- Movement Observed

The cello utilizes muscle groups to produce stabilization, flexion, rotation, and pronation/supination of both upper extremities. Hand and wrist movements include flexion, extension, deviation, abduction, and adduction. Hip position includes flexion, abduction, and external rotation when instrument rests between legs. The degree of movement is greatest in the right shoulder, left elbow, left wrist and left hand. Movement is used to a lesser degree in the left shoulder and right elbow.

Considerations:
- Muscle Strength
- Speed/Dexterity

Muscle strength bilaterally utilized in playing requires extremities to be held up against gravity (Fair+ muscle grade) for periods of time. Additional strength of the left hand is required to depress string or strings, increasing with playing time (Good- to Good muscle grade). Changes in height of string from fingerboard can increase or decrease resistance. The weight of the bow increases the strength requirement of the right hand slightly, with more strength demanded when force is applied in an upward or downward fashion, whether against gravity or not.

The speed/dexterity of the left hand for fingering relies on alternating, upward/downward, and sliding movements with isolated, coupled and mass digit execution. (Plucking with right hand not included.)

Considerations:
- Sensation
- Perception

Playing the cello appears to utilize the deep sensations for arm movements and string depressions, with tactile discrimination required for finger placement. Perceptual components appear to be in the areas of orientation, visual, and motor. (Exclude visual for non-sighted individuals.) Orientation mechanisms direct body movements, using visual cues in a planned and coordinated manner.

Considerations:
- Respiration
- Cardiac Output

The playing of the cello requires moderate exertion (light work), which may increase with prolonged playing. Respiration must be adequate to maintain level of exertion without signs of fatigue.

Considerations:
- Vision
- Audition

The cello may be played by sighted individuals and also by those at any level of visual impairment. (Tactile/kinesthetic modalities may be primarily relied upon.) Auditory levels most functional are in the normal to moderate impairment range.

CELLO

MAJOR MUSCLE GROUPS USED IN PLAYING
WITHOUT SUBSTITUTION OR ADAPTATION

KEY: B=Beginning Level
I=Intermediate Level
A=Advanced Level

P=Held Position for Playing
X=Muscle Movement Used in Playing
•=Increased Usage

Body Part	Function	Muscle or Muscle Groups	Left B	Left I	Left A	Right B	Right I	Right A
Scapula	Stabilization	Serratus Anterior	x			x		
	Abduction	Trapezius (Superior)						
	Elevation	Trapezius (Interior)						
	Depression	Trapezius (Middle)						
	Adduction	Rhomboideus Major & Minor						
Shoulder	Flexion	Deltoideus (Anterior)	p			p		•
	Abduction	Deltoideus (Middle)	x			x	•	x
	Horizontal Adduction	Pectoralis Major						
	External Rotation	External Rotator Group	x	•	•			
	Internal Rotation	Internal Rotator Group	x	•	•	x		•
Elbow	Flexion	Biceps Brachii Brachialis	x			x		
Forearm	Supination	Supinator Group	x	•	•	x		
	Pronation	Pronator Group	x	•	•	p		
Wrist	Deviation, Radial	Flexor Carpi Radial.						
		Extensor Carpi Rad. Longus		x	•	x		
		Extensor Carpi Rad. Brevis						
	Deviation, Ulnar	Flexor Carpi Ulnaris		x	•	x		
		Extensor Carpi Ulnaris						

Body Part	Function	Muscle or Muscle Groups	Left B	I	A	Right B	I	A
	Extension	Extensor Carpi Rad. Longus & Brevis						
		Extensor Carpi Ulnaris	x			x		
	Flexion	Flexor Carpi Radial.						
		Flexor Carpi Ulnaris	x	•	•	x		
Fingers	MP Flexion	Lumbricales	x			p		
	IP Flexion (1st)	Flex. Digit. Superior	x			p		
	IP Flexion (2nd)	Flex.Digit. Prof.	x			p		
	Adduction	Interossei Palmares	x			p		
	Abduction	Interossei Dorsales	x					
	Abduction	Abduct. Digit. Min.	x			p		
Thumb	MP Flexion	Flex. Poll. Brevis	p					
	IP Flexion	Flex. Poll. Longus	p					
	MP Extension	Ext. Poll. Brevis	p					
	Abduction	Abd. Poll. Longus		x		p		
Hip	Flexion	Iliopsoas	p			p		
	Abduction	Fluteus Medius	p			p		
	External Rotation	External Rotator Groups	p			p		

Muscles listed are used in the playing of this instrument; those not listed are not directly involved.

Facial and neck musculature is marked on right and left for convenience.
Increases (•) are noted in Intermediate Level and Advanced Level that are most obvious.
Muscles are used in groups for synergist movements rather than as isolated muscle movements.
Generall, X's in Beginning Level continue in Intermediate and Advanced Levels.

CELLO

These ranges were determined through working with musicians. They reflect the musician's body size, individuality, and possibly style. The ranges are approximate to give a working baseline for instrument suitability.

Head:		Held in a neutral position.
Shoulders:	*Left*	Flexed (60°) with abduction (45 – 90°) and external rotation (–40–60°).
	Right	Flexed (60°) with abduction (0 – 80°) and internal rotation (0 – 40°).
Elbows:	Left	Flexes (80 – 130°) with abduction and rotation.
	Right	Flexes (40 – 90°) with abduction and rotation.
Forearms:	Left	Pronates full range during play with highest degree toward bridge.
	Right	Pronated full range to hold bow.
Wrists:	Left	Flexes (0 – 35°) increasing as hand moves toward bridge.
	Right	Neutral position with ulnar deviation (0 – 100°) at tail of bow and radial deviation (0 – 100°) at tip of bow.
Thumbs:	Left	Abducted (60°) and slides along neck with finger placement.
	Right	Abducted under index finger, holding bow in horizontal plane across palm.
Fingers:	Left	Flex MP (0 – 40°), PIP (0 – 60°), DIP (10 – 60°), with full range of abduction and adduction used during play.
	Right	Held in a flexed and abducted functional fashion, MP (40°), PIP (60°) DIP (40°).
Hips:		Abducted and externally rotated to position instrument.

*i.e., using normal body position for playing, without any devices for instrument or body parts.

Double Bass in normal playing position

Right hand "Pizzicato" technique in play of Double Bass

Left hand position in normal (low-middle register) in play of Double Bass

Left hand position in extreme (upper register) play of Double Bass

Right, Bow hand in "German" grip for Double Bass

Right, Bow hand, in "French" grip for Double Bass

FAMILY: Strings
INSTRUMENT: Acoustic Bass (Upright Bass, String Bass)
SIZE: 3/4
MAKE: Kay
MODEL: Maestro
MATERIALS USED IN CONSTRUCTION: Wood

I. Assembly and Disassembly
The bass and bow are not disassembled by the student although physical manipulation, such as loosening of bow tension, may be required. See *Tuning Requirements* and *Student Maintenance*.

II. Tuning Requirements
Strings are tuned by twisting the geared tuning pegs located at the scroll end of the instrument. Pegs are turned using thumb and second finger of left hand in a clockwise or counterclockwise direction against resistance. This process is usually accomplished with the instrument in playing position. The left hand is used to manipulate pegs on both sides of the scroll while the bow is drawn across the strings with the right hand in order to test for accuracy of intonation.

III. Transport
The instrument is provided with a canvas bag that serves as a protective container and assists transport. The bag is opened by a heavy zipper along its length. A cloth handle is provided near where the body of the instrument slopes toward the neck. The bow is slipped into its own compartment, which is secured by a snap. Weight and dimensional increases are negligible.

IV. Student Maintenance
A. Tuning
The instrument must be tuned both before and during play.
B. Bow Tension
Bow tension may also need to be adjusted during play. This is accomplished by turning an octagonal bolt head 13 mm (.51 inches) in diameter and 28 mm (1.10 inches) in length located at the end of the bow above the frog. The bolt head is gripped between the thumb and second finger and turned in a clockwise or counterclockwise direction against some resistance. Both hands are needed for this operation.
C. Cleaning
The body of the instrument must be cleaned and polished with a soft cloth.
D. Rosining
In order to maintain the necessary friction between bow hair and strings, rosin is applied to the bow. This may be necessary during play and involves the passing of a small bar 60 mm x 30 mm x 20 mm (2.36 x 1.18 x .79 inches) over the hairs. Two hands are needed for this operation.
E. Replacement of Strings
Strings deteriorate with age and break. They may also break owing to overtensioning during the tuning process.

Strings on the instrument examined are known as "ball end" strings. The ball is actually a metal ring which prevents the string from slipping through its opening in the tailpiece. Replacing a string involves threading the plain end through a hole in the tailpiece, routing it over the bridge and nut, and then threading it through another hole located in the tuning peg. The peg is then used to wind up excessive string length (in some instances the string must be cut beforehand). The instrument is then tuned.

V. Variation Among Manufacturers
Dimensions of student grade instruments are similar; however significant modifications such as the addition of an additional string, movement of bridge, and adjustments to string height are possible. Such modifications are made by highly skilled craftsmen and should be undertaken only after careful consideration of a given instrument's value.

Checklist

The following skills are necessary for independence in playing, owning, and receiving instruction on this instrument. The music teacher should confirm the need for those items, such as need for transport, which may not be necessary in all situations. The teacher should also add any items, such as the need to transport instructional materials to and from lessons, which may be applicable.

The therapist should indicate those requirements which a student is able to fulfill. The teacher or parents must provide for assistance in those areas in which a student may be dependent.

	Needed	Can Perform	Can Not Perform
1. Tune instrument	_____	_____	_____
2. Transport instrument	_____	_____	_____
3. Place instrument in case	_____	_____	_____
4. Open and close case	_____	_____	_____
5. Clean instrument	_____	_____	_____
6. Replace broken strings	_____	_____	_____
7. Place instrument in playing position	_____	_____	_____
8. Rosin bow	_____	_____	_____
9. Adjust bow hair tension	_____	_____	_____
10. Adjust endpin	_____	_____	_____

BASS

A full-sized bass was analyzed. The 1/2 and 3/4 basses, when fitted to individual needs, utilize the same basic components as the full size.

Considerations:
- General Body Position
- Major Body Parts Involved in Playing - Mobile/Stable Components - Functions of Major/Minor Joints Involved - Mobile/Stable Capacity

The bass is played in a manner requiring support (*stability*) and movement (*mobility*) of trunk, upper extremities, and lower extremities. The major individual joints that are required to function in a stable capacity are those of the right wrist and hand. Movement is of major importance in joints of shoulders, elbows, left wrist, left hand, and trunk. Joints involved in a minor capacity, but required, are those of the lower extremities for standing posture, balance, and movement.

Considerations:
- Major Muscle Groups
- Movement Observed

The bass utilizes muscle groups to produce stabilization, flexion, abduction, rotation, and pronation/supination of upper extremities. Hand and wrist movements include flexion, extension, deviation, abduction, and adduction. Trunk requirements are rotation, flexion, and extension to maintain posture and allow movement in standing. The degree of movement is greatest in shoulders, left elbow and left hand. Movement is used to a lesser degree in right shoulder, right wrist and trunk.

Considerations:
- Muscle Strength
- Speed/Dexterity

Muscle strength utilized bilaterally in playing the bass requires arms to be held up against gravity (Fair+ muscle grade) for periods of time. Additional strength is required of the left hand to depress string or strings, increasing with playing time (Good- to Good muscle grade). Changes in the height of strings from fingerboard can increase or decrease resistance. The weight of the bow increases the strength requirement of the right hand slightly, with more strength demanded when force is applied in an upward or downward fashion, whether against gravity or not (Good- to Good muscle grade). Strength requirements of lower extremities imply good tone to stand for periods with body movement. The speed/dexterity of the left hand for fingering relies on alternating, up and down, and sliding movements, with isolated, coupled, and mass digit executions increasing with advanced playing.

Considerations:
- Respiration
- Cardiac Output

The playing of the bass requires moderate exertion (light work), which may increase with prolonged playing. Respiration must be adequate to maintain level of exertion without signs of fatigue.

Considerations:
- Vision
- Audition

The bass may be played by sighted individuals and also by those at any level of visual impairment. (Tactile/kinesthetic modalities may be primarily relied upon.) Auditory levels most functional are in the normal to moderate impairment range.

Considerations:
- Sensation
- Perception

Playing the bass appears to utilize the deep sensations for arm movements and depressing strings, with tactile discrimination required for finger placement. Perceptual components appear to be in the areas of orientation, visual and motor. (Exclude visual for non-sighted individuals.) Orientation mechanisms direct body movements using visual cues in a planned, coordinated manner.

BASS

MAJOR MUSCLE GROUPS USED IN PLAYING
WITHOUT SUBSTITUTION OR ADAPTATION

KEY: B=Beginning Level
I =Intermediate Level
A=Advanced Level

P=Held Position for Playing
X=Muscle Movement Used in Playing
• =Increased Usage

Body Part	Function	Muscle or Muscle Groups	Left B	Left I	Left A	Right B	Right I	Right A
Scapula	Elevation	Trapezius (Inferior)	x	—	—	x	—	—
Shoulder	Flexion	Deltoideus (Anterior)	x	•	•	x	—	—
	Abduction	Deltoideus (Middle)	x	—	—	x	•	•
	External Rotation	External Rotator Group	x	—	—	x	—	—
	Internal Rotation	Internal Rotator Group	x	—	—	x	•	•
Elbow	Flexion	Biceps Brachii	x	•	•	x	—	—
		Brachialis						
Forearm	Supination	Supinator Group	x	•	•		—	—
	Pronation	Pronator Group	x	•	•	p	—	—
Wrist	Deviation, Radial	Flexor Carpi Radial.	x	•	•		—	—
		Extensor Carpi Rad. Longus				x		
		Extensor Carpi Rad. Brevis						
	Deviation, Ulnar	Flexor Carpi Ulnaris	x	•	•		—	—
		Extensor Carpi Ulnaris				x		
	Extension	Extensor Carpi Rad. Longus & Brevis	x			x		
		Extensor Carpi Ulnaris						
	Flexion	Flexor Carpi Radial.	x					
		Flexor Carpi Ulnaris				x		

Body Part	Function	Muscle or Muscle Groups	Left B	Left I	Left A	Right B	Right I	Right A
Fingers	MP Flexion	Lumbricales	x	—	—	p	x	•
	IP Flexion (1st)	Flex. Digit. Superior	x	—	—	p	—	—
	IP Flexion (2nd)	Flex. Digit. Prof.	x	—	—	p	—	—
	MP Extension	Ext. Digit. Com.	—	—	—	—	x	•
	Adduction	Interossei Palmares	x	—	—	p	—	—
	Abduction	Interossei Dorsales	x	—	—	p	—	—
		Abduct. Digit. Min.	x	—	—	—	—	—
Thumb	MP Flexion	Flex. Poll. Brevis	—	—	—	p	—	—
	IP Flexion	Flex. Poll. Longus	—	—	—	p	—	—
	Abduction	Abd. Poll. Brevis	—	—	—	p	—	—
		Abd. Poll. Longus	p	—	—	—	—	—
	Adduction	Add. Poll.	x	—	—	—	—	—
Trunk	Flexion	Rectus Abdominis	—	—	—	x	—	—
	Rotation	Obl. Ext. Abdominis	—	—	—	—	—	—
		Obl. Int. Abdominis	x	—	—	x	—	—
	Extension	Thoracic Group	—	—	—	—	—	—
		Lumbar Group	x	—	—	x	—	—
Hip	Flexion	Iliopsoas	x	—	—	x	—	—
Knee	Extension	Quadriceps Femoris	p	—	—	p	—	—

Muscles listed are used in the playing of this instrument; those not listed are not directly involved.

Facial and neck musculature is marked on right and left for convenience.
Increases (•) are noted in Intermediate Level and Advanced Level that are most obvious.
Muscles are used in groups for synergist movements rather than as isolated muscle movements.
Generally X's in Beginning Level continue in Intermediate and Advanced Levels.

BASS

MOVEMENT OBSERVED IN PLAYING
(ACTIVE & POSITIONAL)
WITHOUT SUBSTITUTION OR ADAPTATION*

These ranges were determined through working with musicians. They reflect the musician's body size, individuality, and possibly style. The ranges are approximate to give a working baseline for instrument suitability.

Head:		Neutral position.
Shoulders:	Left	Flexes (20-120°) with abduction (0-110°) and external rotation (60- -60°).
	Right	Flexes (20-45°) with abduction (0-45°) and internal rotation (40-60°).
Elbows:	Left	Flexes (40-120°) with shoulder abducted and externally rotated.
	Right	Flexes (0-20°) with shoulder abducted and internally rotated.
Forearms:	Left	Full range of supination at scroll end (mechanical disadvantage due to shoulder position) and full range of pronation toward bridge.
	Right	Pronated full range with ulnar and radial deviation.
Wrists:	Left	Flexes (60- -20°).
	Right	Extends (20-40°) with ulnar (10°) deviation at tail end of bow.
Thumbs:	Left	Stabilized fingers around neck at (70°) abduction to adduction along side of index finger toward bridge.
	Right	Held in abduction under index finger on bow as in functional resting fashion.
Fingers:	Left	All fingers flex through range minus last 20° at MP's, PIP, and DIP joints utilizing the full range of abduction and adduction during play.
	Right	Fingers held in functional resting fashion with bow placed horizontal to palm MP flexion (45°), PIP flexion (90°), DIP flexion (20°). First and third fingers held in slight abduction to middle phalanx.
Trunk:		Rotates and flexes forward - degree dependent on individual height.
Hips:		As trunk flexes, hips also flex - degree dependent on individual height.

*I.e., using normal body position for playing, without any devices for instrument or body parts.

Acoustic Guitar in normal playing position (Folk-Popular Style)

Acoustic Guitar in normal playing position (Classical Style)

43

Right hand position Plectrum (Pick) technique in play of Guitar

Left hand position in normal play of Guitar

FAMILY: Strings
INSTRUMENT: Acoustic Guitar
TYPE: Steel String   Nylon String
MAKE: Nagoya   Aria
MODEL: F-10   AC-18
MATERIALS USED IN CONSTRUCTION: Wood

Note: Owing to substantial differences in construction and use, acoustic guitars will be compared as subtypes. Nomenclature may differ from manufacturer to manufacturer or even between different localities. Subtypes are as follows:

Steel String Guitars ("Folk or Popular")
These guitars are supplied with six steel strings. Often, a metal reinforcement rod is concealed in the neck. This rod is used to adjust the angle of the neck in relation to the body.

Note: Some steel string guitars, notably those marketed inexpensively, do not have the adjustable reinforcing rod. These inexpensive instruments should be avoided since the wooden neck alone may be subject to warpage and cannot withstand the tension exerted by steel strings. Warpage of the neck will result in increased distance from string to fretboard and render the instrument unplayable.

Nylon String Guitars ("Classical")
These guitars are supplied with three strings of nylon (or gut) composition and three steel strings. The neck is wider and reinforced internally to withstand string tension (tension is less than with all steel strings). The neck is not adjustable. String height is adjusted by modification of string support components (bridge and nut).

Both musical and physical needs must be taken into consideration when considering the relative merits of each type. Extensive variations in body size exist and most manufacturers use a classification based on these criteria.

Picks
The steel string guitar is often played with a pick, and occasionally several smaller finger picks are used. Picks used singly vary in shape, ranging from triangles to tear drop configurations. They are made of various natural or synthetic materials. Single picks are retained in the right hand between the thumb and the side of the second finger. The material used, size, and shape of a pick affect the sound of an instrument. Choice, therefore, depends on musical as well as physical considerations. It should be noted that some picks are available with incised lines or cork at the grasping end in order to prevent slippage. Large felt picks are also used. These picks are similar in all dimensions except thickness. Felt pick thickness may reach 8 mm (.31 inches).

The finger pick is a metal or plastic device placed over individual fingers so that each finger wil function as an individual pick. Generally, the nylon string, or classical guitar is played without a pick, usually with the finger tips or finger nails of the right hand.

I.   Assembly and Disassembly
     The guitar is not disassembled by the student.

II. Tuning Requirements
     Strings are tuned by turning the geared thumbscrews (tuning devices) located at the end of the neck. The thumbscrews are turned by using the thumb and second finger in a clockwise or counterclockwise direction against some resistance. The instrument is maintained in playing position and the right hand sounds each string in order to test accuracy of intonation.

III. Transport
The instruments examined are not sold with cases. This is generally the rule when obtaining guitars. Cases must be purchased as a separate item at additional cost.
   1. Canvas or vinyl bags are available. Weight or dimensional increases are negligible. Bag is opened by large zipper which runs the length of the instrument.
   2. Hard shell cases
      A. Fiber
         These cases add approximately 20 mm (.79 inches) to the outside dimensions of the instrument and an additional 1.5 kg (3.31 lb.) of weight.
      B. Wood Composition
         These cases add as much as 80 mm (3.15 inches) to all outside dimensions and an additional 4.5 kg (9.92 lb.) of weight.
      C. Plastic
         These cases add as much as 80 mm (3.15 inches) to all outside dimensions and an additional 3.5 kg (7.72 lb.) of weight.
      All hard shell cases are opened through the use of three to five latches. Handles are U-shaped.

IV. Student Maintenance
   A. Tuning
      The instrument must be tuned both before and during play.
   B. Cleaning
      The body of the instrument must be cleaned and polished with a soft cloth.
   C. Replacement of strings
      Strings deteriorate with age and break. They may also break owing to the overtensioning during the tuning process or improper use of a pick.
      Steel Strings
      Strings on these instruments are known as "ball end" strings. The ball is actually a small ring which prevents the string from slipping past its retaining pin. The retaining pin is a tapered plastic peg that is wedged into the body of the instrument behind the bridge. These pins are difficult to remove and require an assistive device. The ball end is dropped into the hole and the pin replaced. The string is then routed over the bridge and nut and threaded through a hole in the tuning machine. The tuning machines are then used to wind up excessive string length (in some cases the string must be cut). The instrument is then tuned.
      Nylon Strings
      The process is similar except that the instrument does not have retaining pins. The plain end of the string is threaded through a hole located behind or in the bridge. The ball end cannot fit through the hole.

V. Variation Among Manufacturers
   A. Guitars are available in a wide range of body styles, each of which is designed to fulfill a specific musical purpose.
   B. Strings
      Strings are available in several gauges, which may be greater or smaller than those on the instruments examined. They are also made in a variety of materials, which alter the sound and playing characteristics of an instrument. Some nylon string guitars require the use of plain, or straight end, strings. Replacement involves threading these strings through a small hole and tying a special knot.
   C. Straps
      The weight of the instrument is often supported by a strap. Straps may be of leather, plastic (vinyl), or cloth construction. They are attached to the bottom of the instrument and the end located near the tuning mechanism. Straps are usually placed over the left shoulder and used in both sitting and standing positions.

VI. Other Devices
   A. Footrests
      Footrests are designed to raise the level of the right leg as much as 200 mm (7.87 inches) above the floor. This may help to maintain the instrument in a proper playing position when sitting.
   B. The capo
      The capo may be used to raise the pitch of an instrument by depressing strings at a given fret. All capos have a bar which is placed across the strings, but the means of applying and maintaining pressure varies. Some use thick pieces of elastic; others use a cam action. The amount of strength and motor control needed to install a capo in position depends upon the mechanism of the individual manufacturer. Several types should be examined if musical need dictates their use.

Instrument: Acoustic Guitar

Checklist

The following skills are necessary for independence in playing, owning, and receiving instruction on this instrument. The music teacher should confirm the need for those items, such as need for transport, which may not be necessary in all situations. The teacher should also add any items, such as the need to transport instructional materials to and from lessons, which may be applicable.

The therapist should indicate those requirements which a student is able to fulfill. The teacher or parents must provide for assistance in those areas in which a student may be dependent.

	Needed	Can Perform	Can Not Perform
1. Tune instrument	———	———	———
2. Transport instrument	———	———	———
3. Place instrument in case	———	———	———
4. Open and close case	———	———	———
5. Clean instrument	———	———	———
6. Replace broken strings	———	———	———
7. Place instrument in playing position	———	———	———
8. Attach shoulder strap	———	———	———
9. Adjust footrest	———	———	———
10. Grasp pick	———	———	———
11. Retrieve dropped pick	———	———	———
12. Adjust capo	———	———	———

GUITAR (6-String Acoustic)

Considerations:
- General Body Position
- Major Body Parts Involved in Playing - Mobile/Stable Components - Functions of Major/Minor Joints Involved - Mobile/ Stable Capacity

The acoustic guitar is played in a manner requiring support (stability) and movement (mobility) of trunk and both upper extremities. The major individual joints that are required to function in a stable capacity are the right shoulder, right elbow, and right wrist. Movement is of major importance in joints of the left shoulder, left elbow, left wrist, and fingers of the left and right hands.

Considerations:
- Major Muscle Groups
- Movement Observed

The acoustic guitar utilizes muscle groups to produce stabilization, flexion, rotation, abduction, pronation, and supination. Hand and wrist movements include flexion, extension, deviation, abduction, and adduction. The degree of movement is greatest for the left shoulder, left elbow, left wrist, and fingers bilaterally.

Considerations:
- Muscle Strength
- Speed/Dexterity

Muscle strength utilized bilaterally in playing the acoustic guitar requires holding arms up against gravity (Fair+ muscle grade) for periods of time. Additional strength is required of the left hand to depress string or strings increasing with playing time (Good- to Good muscle grade). Changes of height of strings from fingerboard can increase or decrease resistance. Right hand strength requirements increase with demands of fingering (Good- muscle grade). The speed/dexterity of the left hand for fingering relies on rapid alternating up/down movements with isolated, coupled, and mass digit execution, increasing with advanced playing. The right hand utilizes alternating, finger rolling executions, increasing with advanced playing.

Considerations:
- Sensation
- Perception

Playing the acoustic guitar appears to utilize the deep sensations for arm movements and depressing strings, with tactile discrimination required for finger placement and strumming. Perceptual components appear to be in the areas of orientation, visual and motor. (Exclude visual for non-sighted individuals). Orientation mechanisms direct body movements using visual cues in a planned coordinated manner.

Considerations:
- Respiration
- Cardiac Output

The playing of the acoustic guitar requires moderate exertion (light work) which may increase with prolonged playing. Respiration must be adequate to maintain level of exertion without signs of fatigue.

Considerations:
- Vision
- Audition

The acoustic guitar may be played by sighted individuals and also by those at any level of visual impairment. (Tactile/kinesthetic modalities may be primarily relied upon.) Auditory levels most functional are in the normal to moderate impairment range.

GUITAR (6 String Acoustic)

MAJOR MUSCLE GROUPS USED IN PLAYING
WITHOUT SUBSTITUTION OR ADAPTATION

KEY: B=Beginning Level   P=Held Position for Playing
            I =Intermediate Level   X=Muscle Movement Used in Playing
            A=Advanced Level   • =Increased Usage

Body Part	Function	Muscle or Muscle Groups	Left B	Left I	Left A	Right B	Right I	Right A
Scapula	Elevation	Trapezius (Inferior)	p			p		
Shoulder	Flexion	Deltoideus (Anterior)	x			x		
	Abduction	Deltoideus (Middle)	x	•	•	p		
	External Rotation	External Rotator Group	x	•	•			
	Internal Rotation	Internal Rotator Group	x	•	•	p		
Elbow	Flexion	Biceps Brachii	x					
		Brachialis				p		
Forearm	Supination	Supinator Group	x	•	•			
	Pronation	Pronator Group	x			p		
Wrist	Deviation, Radial	Flexor Carpi Radial.	x					
		Extensor Carpi Rad. Longus	x					
		Extensor Carpi Rad. Brevis						
	Deviation, Ulnar	Flexor Carpi Ulnaris	x	•	•			
	Extension	Extensor Carpi Ulnaris						
		Extensor Carpi Rad. Longus & Brevis						
		Extensor Carpi Radial.	x					
	Flexion	Flexor Carpi Radial.						
		Flexor Carpi Ulnaris	x			p		

Body Part	Function	Muscle or Muscle Groups	Left			Right		
			B	I	A	B	I	A
Fingers	MP Flexion	Lumbricales	x	—	—	x	—	—
	IP Flexion (1st)	Flex. Digit. Superior	x	—	—	x	—	—
	IP Flexion (2nd)	Flex. Digit. Prof.	x	—	—	x	—	—
	MP Extension	Ext. Digit. Com.		—	—	x	—	—
	Adduction	Interossei Palmares	x	—	—	x	—	—
	Adduction	Interossei Dorsales	x	—	—	x	—	—
	Abduction	Abduct. Digit. Min.	x	—	—	x	—	—
Thumb	MP Flexion	Flex. Poll. Brevis	—	—	—	x	—	—
	IP Flexion	Flex. Poll. Longus	—	—	—	p	—	—
	MP Extension	Ext. Poll. Brevis	—	—	—	x	—	—
	Abduction	Abd. Poll. Brevis	x	—	—	x	—	—
	Abduction	Abd. Poll. Longus	—	—	—		—	—

Muscles listed are used in the playing of this instrument; those not listed are not directly involved.

Facial and neck musculature is marked on right and left for convenience.
Increases (•) are noted in Intermediate Level and Advanced Level that are most obvious.
Muscles are used in groups for synergist movements rather than as isolated muscle movements.
Generally, X's in Beginning Level continue in Intermediate and Advanced Levels.

GUITAR (6-String Acoustic)

MOVEMENT OBSERVED IN PLAYING
(ACTIVE & POSITIONAL)
WITHOUT SUBSTITUTION OR ADAPTATION*

These ranges were determined through working with musicians. They reflect the musician's body size, individuality, and possibly style. The ranges are approximate to give a working baseline for instrument suitability.

Head:		Held in neutral position.
Shoulders:	Left	Flexed (20°) and abducts (0–45°) with external rotation (0–30°).
	Right	Flexed (20°) and abducts (30°) with internal rotation (60°).
Elbows:	Left	Flexes (90–120°) with shoulder abduction and rotation.
	Right	Flexed (90°) with shoulder abduction and rotation.
Forearms:	Left	Supinates (60–90°).
	Right	Pronated full range.
Wrists:	Left	Flexes (20–45°) with ulnar deviation (0–30°).
	Right	Flexed (20°).
Thumbs:	Left	Abducted (60°) opposite index finger around neck.
	Right	Abducted to index finger and flexes (0–20°).
Fingers:	Left	Flex MP (0–30°), PIP (45–90°), DIP (0–90°), with abduction and adduction used during play.
	Right	Flex MP (20–60°), PIP (45–90°), DIP (0–90°).

*I.e., using normal body position for playing, without any devices for instrument or body use.

FAMILY: Strings
INSTRUMENT: Guitar
TYPE: Electric
MAKE: Fender
MODEL: Stratocaster
MATERIALS USED IN CONSTRUCTION: Wood

Picks
The electric guitar is usually played with a pick. Picks vary in shape ranging from triangles to tear drop configurations. They are made of various natural or synthetic materials. A single pick is retained in the left hand between the thumb and the side of the second finger. The material used, size, and shape of pick affect the sound of an instrument, and choice is, therefore, a musical as well as physical consideration. It should be noted that some picks are available with incised lines or cork at the grasping end in order to prevent slippage.

I. Assembly and Disassembly
The guitar is not disassembled by the student. However, it must be connected to a source of amplification. This connection is made by a cord with phone type plugs. One end of the cord is inserted in the amplifier and a socket is located in the body of the instrument to receive the other end. See Section VII, Item B.

II. Tuning Requirements
Strings are tuned by turning the geared thumbscrews (tuning devices) located at the end of the neck. The tuning devices are operated by using the thumb and second finger in a clockwise or counterclockwise direction against some resistance. The instrument is maintained in playing position and the pick hand (usually the right) sounds each string in order to test accuracy of intonation.

III. Transport
The instrument examined is not sold with a case. This is generally the rule when obtaining guitars. Cases must usually be purchased as a separate item at additional cost.
1. Canvas or vinyl bags are available. Weight or dimensional increases are negligible. Bag is opened by a large zipper which runs the length of the instrument.
2. Hard shell cases
    A. Fiber
        These cases add approximately 20 mm (.79 inches) to the outside dimensions of an instrument and an additional weight of approximately 1.5 kg (3.31 lb.).
    B. Wood composition
        These cases add as much as 80 mm (3.15 inches) to all outside dimensions and an additional 4.5 kg. (9.92 lb.) of weight.
    C. Plastic
        These cases add as much as 80 mm (3.15 inches) to all outside dimensions and an additional 3.5 kg (7.72 lb.) of weight.
    All hard shell cases are opened through the use of latches. Handles are U-shaped.

IV. Student Maintenance
    A. Tuning
        The instrument must be tuned both before and during play.
    B. Cleaning
        The instrument must be cleaned and polished with a soft cloth.
    C. Replacement of Strings
        Strings deteriorate with age and break. They may also break owing to overtensioning during the tuning process or improper use of a pick. Strings on the instrument examined are known as "ball end" strings. This type of string is generally the rule on electric guitars. The ball is actually a small ring which prevents the string from

slipping through a hole drilled through the body of the instrument. Strings are replaced by passing the plain end through one of these holes, beginning at the back of the instrument. The string is then routed over the bridge and nut and threaded through a hole in the tuning device. The tuning devices are then used to wind up excessive string length (in some cases the string must be cut). The instrument is then tuned.

D. Tone Adjustments
The electric guitar examined has three knobs 17 mm (7 inches) in diameter and a three-position toggle switch located on the front of the instrument. These controls are used to adjust the sound of the instrument and may be used during play.

E. Adjustable bridges
Each string is mounted on an individually adjusted bridge. These bridges are used to adjust string height or length.

V. Variation Among Manufacturers
A. Electric guitars are available in a wide range of body styles, each of which is designed to fulfill a specific music purpose.

B. Strings
Strings are available in several gauges, which may be greater or smaller than those on the instrument examined.

C. Straps
The weight of the instrument is usually supported by a strap. Straps may be of leather, plastic (vinyl), or cloth construction. They are attached to the bottom of the instrument and the end near the tuning mechanism. Straps are usually placed over the left shoulder and used in both sitting and standing positions.

VI. Other Devices
A. Footrests
Footrests are designed to raise the level of the right leg as much as 200 mm (7.87 inches) above the floor. This may help to maintain the instrument in a proper playing position when seated.

B. Amplifiers
The preceding data has not taken the means of amplification into consideration since this is not a playing component of the instrument. Amplification is necessary if the instrument is to produce sound. The amplifier may not need to be manipulated by the student during play since controls are located on the instrument body. If manipulation of controls is needed, or desired, then available units should be examined in order to determine the student's ability to reach and adjust individual controls. Pedals are marketed which may enable the student to modify tone in various ways through foot and ankle movement while playing.

Checklist

The following skills are necessary for independence in playing, owning, and receiving instruction on this instrument. The music teacher should confirm the need for those items, such as need for transport, which may not be necessary in all situations. The teacher should also add any items, such as the need to transport instructional materials to and from lessons, which may be applicable.

The therapist should indicate those requirements which a student is able to fulfill. The teacher or parents must provide for assistance in those areas in which a student may be dependent.

	Needed	Can Perform	Can Not Perform
1. Tune instrument	_____	_____	_____
2. Transport instrument	_____	_____	_____
3. Place instrument in case	_____	_____	_____
4. Open and close case	_____	_____	_____
5. Clean instrument	_____	_____	_____
6. Replace broken strings	_____	_____	_____
7. Place instrument in playing position	_____	_____	_____
8. Attach shoulder strap	_____	_____	_____
9. Adjust footrest	_____	_____	_____
10. Grasp pick	_____	_____	_____
11. Retrieve dropped pick	_____	_____	_____
12. Attach cord from instrument to amplifier	_____	_____	_____
13. Manipulate controls on instrument	_____	_____	_____
14. Turn AC power on and off	_____	_____	_____
15. Adjust capo	_____	_____	_____

GUITAR (6-String Electric)

Considerations:
- General Body Position
- Major Body Parts Involved in Playing - Mobile/Stable Components - Functions of Major/Minor Joints Involved - Mobile/Stable Capacity

The electric guitar is played in a manner requiring support *(stability)* of the trunk, and movement *(mobility)* of both upper extremities. The major individual joints that are required to function in a stable capacity are those of the right shoulder, right thumb, and right index finger *(note:* pick playing), and left thumb. Movement is of major importance in joints of the left shoulder, right and left elbows, right and left wrists, and fingers of the left hand.

Considerations:
- Major Muscle Groups
- Movement Observed

This guitar utilizes muscle groups to produce stability, flexion, and abduction of upper extremities. Hand and wrist use involves flexion, extension, deviation, abduction, and adduction. Movement is greatest for the left shoulder, left wrist, and fingers of the left hand. Movement is used to a lesser degree in the right elbow and wrist.

Considerations:
- Muscle Strength
- Speed/Dexterity

Muscle strength utilized in playing the guitar requires that arms be help up against gravity (Fair+ muscle grade) for periods of time. Additional strength is required for the left hand for depressing the string or strings (Good- to Good muscle grade). Changes of height of strings from fingerboard can increase or decrease resistance. The speed/dexterity of the left hand for fingering relies on rapid alternating, sliding, up/down movements with isolated, coupled, and mass digit execution, increasing with advanced playing. The right hand relies (pick playing) on fine wrist adjustments.

Considerations:
- Sensation
- Perception

Playing the guitar appears to utilize the deep sensations for arm movements and depressing strings, with tactile discrimination needed for finger placement. Perceptual components appear to be in the areas of orientation, visual and motor. (Exclude visual for non-sighted individuals). Orientation mechanisms direct body movements using visual cues in a planned coordinated manner.

Considerations:
- Respiration
- Cardiac Output

Playing the guitar requires moderate exertion (light work) which may increase with prolonged playing. Respiration must be adequate to maintain exertion without signs of fatigue.

Considerations:
- Vision
- Audition

The guitar may be played by sighted individuals and also by those at any level of visual impairment. (Tactile/kinesthetic modalities may be primarily relied upon.) Auditory levels most functional are normal to moderate impairment.

GUITAR (6-String Electric)

MAJOR MUSCLE GROUPS USED IN PLAYING
WITHOUT SUBSTITUTION OR ADAPTATION

KEY:
B=Beginning Level
I =Intermediate Level
A=Advanced Level

P=Held Position for Playing
X=Muscle Movement Used in Playing
•=Increased Usage

Body Part	Function	Muscle or Muscle Groups	Left B	Left I	Left A	Right B	Right I	Right A
Scapula	Elevation	Trapezius (Inferior)	x			x		
Shoulder	Flexion	Deltoideus (Anterior)	p			p		
	Abduction	Deltoideus (Middle)	x	•	•	p		
	Horizontal Abduction	Deltoideus (Post.)						
	Horizontal Adduction	Pectoralis (Major)	x			x		
	External Rotation	External Rotator Group		•	•			
	Internal Rotation	Internal Rotator Group				p		
Elbow	Flexion	Biceps Brachii	x			x		
		Brachialis						
Forearm	Supination	Supinator Group	x					
	Pronation	Pronator Group	x			p		
Wrist	Deviation, Radial	Flexor Carpi Radial.	x					
		Extensor Carpi Rad. Longus				x		
		Extensor Carpi Rad. Brevis						
	Deviation, Ulnar	Flexor Carpi Ulnaris						
		Extensor Carpi Ulnaris	x	•	•	x		
	Extension	Extensor Carpi Rad. Longus & Brevis						
		Extensor Carpi Ulnaris	x			x		
	Flexion	Flexor Carpi Radial.	x			x		
		Flexor Carpi Ulnaris	x			x		

Body Part	Function	Muscle or Muscle Groups	Left B	Left I	Left A	Right B	Right I	Right A
Fingers	MP Flexion	Lumbricales	x	—	—	p	—	—
	IP Flexion (1st)	Flex. Digit. Superior	x	—	—	p	—	—
	IP Flexion (2nd)	Flex. Digit. Prof.	x	—	—	p	—	—
	MP Extension	Ext. Digit. Com.	x	—	—	—	—	—
	Adduction	Interossei Palmares	x	—	—	—	—	—
	Abduction	Interossei Dorsales	x	—	—	—	—	—
		Abduct. Digit. Min.	x	—	—	—	—	—
Thumb	Abduction	Abd. Poll. Brevis	p	—	—	—	—	—
		Abd. Poll. Longus	—	—	—	p	—	—
Hip	Flexion	Iliopsoas*	—	—	—	p	—	—
*Foot Rest								

Muscles listed are used in the playing of this instrument; those not listed are not directly involved.

Facial and neck musculature is marked on right and left for convenience.
Increases (●) are noted in Intermediate and Advanced Levels that are most obvious.
Muscles are used in groups for synergist movements rather than as isolated muscle movements.
Generally, X's in Beginning Level continue in Intermediate and Advanced Levels.

GUITAR (6-String Electric)

MOVEMENT OBSERVED IN PLAYING
(ACTIVE & POSITIONAL)
WITHOUT SUBSTITUTION OR ADAPTATION*

These ranges were determined through working with musicians. They reflect the musician's body size, individuality, and possibly style. The ranges are approximate to give a working baseline for instrument suitability.

Head:		Held in neutral position.
Shoulders:	Left	Flexed (10°) and abducts (0–30°) with external rotation (0–40°).
	Right	Flexed (20°) and abduction (30°) with internal rotation (45°).
Elbows:	Left	Flexes (80-90°) with shoulder abduction and rotation.
	Right	Flexes (90-95°) with shoulder abduction and rotation.
Forearms:	Left	Supinates (80-90°).
	Right	Pronated full range.
Wrists:	Left	Flexes (0–45°) with ulnar deviation (0–30°).
	Right	Flexes (0–20°) with ulnar deviation (0–30°) and radial deviation (0–20°) with strumming.
Thumbs:	Left	Abducted (60°) opposite index finger around neck.
	Right	Abducted to index finger for pick playing.
Fingers:	Left	Flex - MP (0–60°), PIP (40–90°), DIP (60–90°), with abduction and adduction used during play.
	Right	Positioned in functional hand fashion except index, which holds pick. Index flexed: MP (30°), PIP (90°), DIP (60°). 3rd,4th,5th flexed: MP (30°), PIP (45°), DIP (30°).

*I.e., using normal body position for playing without any devices for instrument or body parts.

Electric Bass Guitar in normal playing position

AUGUSTANA UNIVERSITY COLLEGE
LIBRARY

Left hand position in normal play of Electric Bass Guitar

Right hand position in normal play of Electric Bass Guitar

FAMILY: Strings
INSTRUMENT: Bass
TYPE: Electric
MAKE: Fender
MODEL: Mustang
MATERIALS USED IN CONSTRUCTION: Wood

I. Assembly and Disassembly

The bass is not disassembled by the student. However, it must be connected to a source of amplification. This connection is made by a cord with phone type plugs. One end of the cord is inserted in the amplifier and a socket is located in the body of the instrument to receive the other end. See Section VI, Item B.

II. Tuning Requirements

Strings are tuned by turning the geared thumbscrews (tuning devices) located at the end of the neck. The thumbscrews are operated by using the thumb and second finger in a clockwise or counterclockwise direction against some resistance. The instrument is maintained in playing position and the right hand sounds each string in order to test accuracy of intonation.

III. Transport

The instrument examined is not sold with a case. This is generally the rule when obtaining a bass. Cases must usually be purchased as a separate item at additional cost.

1. Canvas or vinyl bags are available. Weight or dimensional increases are negligible. Bag is opened by a large zipper running the length of the instrument.
2. Hard shell cases
    A. Fiber

    These cases add approximately 20 mm (.8 inches) to the outside dimensions of an instrument and an additional weight of approximately 1.5 kg (3.3 lb.).
    B. Wood composition

    These cases add as much as 80 mm (3.1 inches) to all outside dimensions and an additional 4.5 kg (9.9 lb.) of weight.
    C. Plastic

    These cases add as much as 80 mm (3.1 inches) to all outside dimensions and an additional 3.5 kg (7.7 lb.) of weight.

All hard shell cases are opened through the use of latches. Handles are U-shaped.

IV. Student Maintenance

A. Tuning

The instrument must be tuned both before and during play.
B. Cleaning

The instrument must be cleaned and polished with a soft cloth.
C. Replacement of strings

Strings deteriorate with age and break. They may also break owing to overtensioning during the tuning process. Strings on the instrument examined are known as "ball end" strings. This type of string is generally the rule on the electric bass. The ball is actually a small ring which prevents the string from slipping through a hole drilled through the body of the instrument. Strings are replaced by passing the plain end through one of these holes, beginning at the back of the instrument. The string is then routed over the bridge and nut and threaded through a hole in the tuning device. The tuning devices are then used to wind up excessive string length (in some cases the string must be cut). The instrument is then tuned.
D. Tone adjustments

The electric bass examined has two knobs 20 mm (.8 inches) in diameter and a three-position toggle switch located on the front of the instrument. These controls are used to adjust the sound of the instrument and may be used during play.

E. Adjustable bridges
   Each string is mounted on an individually adjusted bridge. These bridges may be used to adjust string height or length.

V. Variation Among Manufacturers
   A. Instruments are available in a wide range of body styles, each of which is designed to fulfill a specific musical purpose.
   B. Strings
      Strings are available in several gauges, which may be greater or smaller than those on the instrument examined.
   C. Straps
      The weight of the instrument is usually supported by a strap. Straps may be of leather, plastic (vinyl), or cloth construction. They are attached to the bottom of the instrument and the end near the tuning mechanism. Straps are usually placed over the left shoulder and used in both sitting and standing positions.

VI. Other Devices
   A. Footrests
      Footrests are designed to raise the level of the right leg as much as 200 mm (7.9 inches) above the floor. This may help to maintain the instrument in a proper playing position when seated.
   B. Amplifiers
      The preceding data has not taken the means of amplification into consideration since this is not a playing component of the instrument. Amplification is necessary if the instrument is to produce sound. The amplifier may not need to be manipulated by the student during play since controls are located on the instrument body. If manipulation of controls is needed or desired, available units should be examined in order to determine the student's ability to reach and adjust individual controls. Pedals are marketed that may enable the student to modify tone in various ways through foot and ankle movement while playing.

Checklist

The following skills are necessary for independence in playing, owning, and receiving instruction on this instrument. The music teacher should confirm the need for those items, such as need for transport, which may not be necessary in all situations. The teacher should also add any items, such as the need to transport instructional materials to and from lessons, which may be applicable.

The therapist should indicate those requirements which a student is able to fulfill. The teacher or parents must provide for assistance in those areas in which a student may be dependent.

	Needed	Can Perform	Can Not Perform
1. Tune instrument	————	————	————
2. Transport instrument	————	————	————
3. Place instrument in case	————	————	————
4. Open and close case	————	————	————
5. Clean instrument	————	————	————
6. Replace broken strings	————	————	————
7. Place instrument in playing position	————	————	————
8. Attach shoulder strap	————	————	————
9. Adjust footrest	————	————	————
10. Attach cord from instrument to amplifier	————	————	————
11. Manipulate controls on instrument	————	————	————
12. Turn AC power on and off	————	————	————

ELECTRIC BASS GUITAR

Considerations:
- General Body Position
- Major Body Parts Involved in Playing - Mobile/Stable Components - Functions of Major/Minor Joints Involved - Mobile/Stable Capacity

The electric bass is played in a manner requiring support *(stability)* and movement *(mobility)* of the trunk and both upper extremities. The major individual joints required to function in a stable capacity are those of the trunk, right shoulder, left elbow and thumbs bilaterally. Movement is of major importance in joints of the left shoulder, left wrist, left fingers, and first three fingers of the right hand.

Considerations:
- Major Muscle Groups
- Movement Observed

The electric bass utilizes muscle groups to produce stabilization, flexion, abduction, rotation, pronation, and supination of both upper extremities. Hand and wrist movements include flexion, extension, deviation, abduction, and adduction. The degree of movement is greatest for the left shoulder, left wrist, fingers of the left hand, and first three fingers of the right hand. Movement is used to a lesser degree in the right elbow.

Considerations:
- Muscle Strength
- Speed/Dexterity

Muscle strength utilized bilaterally in playing the electric bass requires holding arms up against gravity (Fair+ muscle grade) for periods of time. Additional strength is required of the left hand to depress string or strings, increasing with playing time (Good- to Good muscle grade). Changes of height of strings from fingerboard can increase or decrease resistance. Right hand fingering strength requires exertion to strike strings in a repetitive nature (Good- to Good muscle grade). The speed/dexterity of the left hand for fingering relies on rapid alternating up and down, and sliding movements with isolated, coupled, and at times mass finger execution. The speed/dexterity of the right hand utilizes independent finger rolling executions in an up/down manner.

Considerations:
- Sensation
- Perception

The electric bass appears to utilize the deep sensations for arm movements and depressing strings, with tactile discrimination needed for finger placement and strumming. Perceptual components appear to be in the areas of orientation, visual and motor. (Exclude visual for non-sighted individuals). Orientation mechanisms direct body movements using visual cues in a planned coordinated manner.

Considerations:
- Respiration
- Cardiac Output

The playing of the electric bass requires moderate exertion (light work), which may increase with prolonged playing. Respiration must be adequate to maintain the level of exertion without signs of fatigue.

Considerations:
- Vision
- Audition

The electric bass may be played by sighted individuals and also by those at any level of visual impairment. (Tactile/kinesthetic modalities may be primarily relied upon.) Auditory levels most functional are in the normal to moderate impairment range.

ELECTRIC BASS GUITAR

MAJOR MUSCLE GROUPS USED IN PLAYING
WITHOUT SUBSTITUTION OR ADAPTATION

KEY: B=Beginning Level
I =Intermediate Level
A=Advanced Level

P=Held Position for Playing
X=Muscle Movement Used in Playing
•=Increased Usage

Body Part	Function	Muscle or Muscle Groups	Left B	Left I	Left A	Right B	Right I	Right A
Scapula	Elevation	Trapezius (Inferior)	x			x		
Shoulder	Flexion	Deltoideus (Anterior)	p			p		
	Abduction	Deltoideus (Middle)	x	•	•	p		
	External Rotation	External Rotator Group	x					
	Internal Rotation	Internal Rotator Group	x	•	•	p		
Elbow	Flexion	Biceps Brachii	x			p		
		Brachialis						
Forearm	Supination	Supinator Group	p					
	Pronation	Pronator Group				p		
Wrist	Deviation, Radial	Flexor Carpi Radial.	x					
		Extensor Carpi Rad. Longus						
		Extensor Carpi Rad. Brevis						
	Deviation, Ulnar	Flexor Carpi Ulnaris	x			p		
	Extension	Extensor Carpi Rad. Longus & Brevis	x					
		Extensor Carpi Ulnaris				p		
	Flexion	Flexor Carpi Radial.	x			x		
		Flexor Carpi Ulnaris	x	•	•	x		

Body Part	Function	Muscle or Muscle Groups	Left B	Left I	Left A	Right B	Right I	Right A
Fingers	MP Flexion	Lumbricales	x	—	—	x	—	—
	IP Flexion (1st)	Flex. Digit. Superior	x	—	—	x	—	—
	IP Flexion (2nd)	Flex. Digit. Prof.	x	—	—	x	—	—
	MP Extension	Ext. Digit. Com.	x	—	—	x	—	—
	Adduction	Interossei Palmares	x	—	—	x	—	—
	Abduction	Interossei Dorsales	x	—	—	—	—	—
		Abduct. Digit. Min.	x	—	—	—	—	—
	Opposition	Opponens Digit. Min.	—	—	—	—	—	—
Thumb	Abduction	Abd. Poll. Longus	p	—	—	—	—	—
	Adduction	Abd. Poll.	—	—	—	p	—	—

Facial and neck musculature is marked on right and left for convenience.
Increases (•) are noted in Intermediate Level and Advanced Level that are most obvious.
Muscles are used in groups for synergist movements rather than as isolated muscle movements.
Generally, X's in Beginning Level continue in Intermediate and Advanced Levels.

ELECTRIC BASS GUITAR (without pick)

MOVEMENT OBSERVED IN PLAYING
(ACTIVE & POSITIONAL)
WITHOUT SUBSTITUTION OR ADAPTATION*

These ranges were determined through working with musicians. They reflect the musician's body size, individuality, and possibly style. The ranges are approximate to give a working baseline for instrument suitability.

Head:		Held in neutral position.
Shoulders:	Left	Flexes (20°) and abducts (0–60°) with internal rotation (0–60°).
	Right	Flexed (10°) and abducted (50°) with internal rotation (30°).
Elbows:	Left	Flexed (90°) with shoulder movements.
	Right	Flexes (90–100°) with shoulder position.
Forearms:	Left	Supinated full range.
	Right	Pronated full range.
Wrists:	Left	Flexes (30–45°) with ulnar deviation (0–30°) used during play.
	Right	Flexed (30°) with ulnar deviation (20°) held while fingering.
Thumbs:	Left	Abducted (60°) around neck of guitar.
	Right	Abducted (passive) along side of index.
Fingers:	Left	Flex - MP (0–30°), PIP (40–90°), DIP (20–90°); abduction and adduction used during play.
	Right	Use 2nd, 3rd, and at times, 4th fingers. Flex - MP (60–90°), PIP (0–90°), DIP (20–40°), adduction of fingers used during play.

*I.e., using normal body position for playing, without any devices for instrument or body parts.

FAMILY: BRASS

INSTRUMENTS: B-Flat TRUMPET

FRENCH HORN

TROMBONE

INTRODUCTION

Brass instruments are basically long tubes, with either conical or cylindrical bores, a flared bell, and a cup-shaped mouthpiece. Any one of the brass instruments would exceed ten feet in length if the tubing were not convoluted.

The sounding agent of brass instruments is the player's lips, which vibrate in response to the player's forcing air through them. They, in turn, cause the air column within the instrument to vibrate, producing a tone.

Open or natural brass instruments can sound several pitches by reacting to a change in frequency of vibration of the player's lips. The player of the trumpet and French horn can also change pitch by means of valves which re-route the air column through different length tubes of the instrument, changing the resonating length of the column and, therefore, the pitch. The trombonist accomplishes this change in resonating length by literally altering the total length of the instrument by means of a slide.

BRASS INSTRUMENTS
SPECIAL CONSIDERATIONS

As mentioned, these instruments have a cup-shaped mouthpiece which varies in depth and width of brim acording to the size of the instrument.

Instruments: Trombone (with F attachment) - Large Cup-Shaped Mouthpiece
                      Trumpet (B-flat) - Small Cup-Shaped Mouthpiece
                      French Horn (F Single) - Small Cup-Shaped Mouthpiece

Considerations: • Embouchure

The lips are drawn back into a tensed position and the mouthpiece is placed lightly against both upper and lower lips. The lower jaw is shifted downward and forward with the upper and lower incisors slightly apart to permit flow of air stream. Ideally, the incisors support the upper and lower lips with equal pressure.

Considerations: • Facial Muscles Involved

The muscles involved in order of importance are: the orbicularis oris, caninus, trangularis, quadratus labii superioris, quadratus labii inferioris, zygomaticus, risorius, mentalis, buccinator, masseter, platysma, supra and infrahyoid muscles.

Considerations: • Dental Occlusion/Dental Irregularities

Instruments are contraindicated if the individual has the following occlusions:

        Class I with Complications
        Class II, Division II
        Most of Class III

Instruments may be contraindicated by these occlusions:

        Class II, Division I-If the upper and lower teeth are not in alignment when the jaw is protruded.
        Class I-With protruding incisors.

The following dental irregularities may affect ability to form proper embouchure:

        Maxillary protrusion
        Low anterior crowding
        Extreme open bites
        Single maxillary central or lateral incisor in linguoversion to its opponent in the mandibular arch.

Considerations: • Respiration

Normal vital capacity is recommended. The preferred method of breathing is diaphragmatic. The pattern of breathing is rapid inspiration followed by shorter expirations owing to larger air flow rate. Several inspirations in quick succession for fortissimo playing.

INSTRUMENT SELECTION GUIDE

An "X" indicates a potential physical limitation in relationship to "normal" use of the instrument. The presence of an "X" should not necessarily preclude consideration of the instrument if compensatory techniques and adaptations are appropriate.

Potential Limitations	B-flat Trumpet	French Horn	Trombone
Contractures of			
Neck	X	X	X
Shoulder	X	X	X
Elbows	X	X	X
Wrists	X	X	X
Fingers	X	X	X
Hips			
Knees			
Ankles			
Incoordination			
Gross - Upper Extremities			X
- Lower Extremities			
Fine - Upper Extremities	X	X	
- Lower Extremities			
Limb Loss (prosthesis fit implied)			
- Upper Extremities			
- Above Elbow	X	X	X
- Below Elbow	X	X	X
- Partial Hand	X	X	X
Lower Extremities			
- Above Knee			
- Below Knee			
- Symes			
- Partial Foot			
- Hip Disarticulation			

Potential Limitations	B-flat Trumpet	French Horn	Trombone
Movement			
Athetoid - Upper Extremities	X	X	X
- Lower Extremities			
Rigidity - Upper Extremities	X	X	X
- Lower Extremities			
Fluctuating Tone			
- Upper Extremities	X	X	X
- Lower Extremities			
Tremor			
Resting - Upper Extremities	X	X	X
Intention - Upper Extremities	X	X	X
Dysmetria	X	X	X
Pain	X	X	X
Perception - Children			
Apraxia	X	X	X
Posture & Bilateral Integration	X	X	X
Space Visual			X
- Adult			
Neglect	X	X	X
Hemianopsia	X	X	X
Spatial	X	X	X
Apraxia	X	X	X

Potential Limitations		B-flat Trumpet	French Horn	Trombone
Sensation				
	Tactile	X	X	X
	Proprioception	X	X	X
	Kinesthesia	X	X	X
Spasticity	- Upper Extremities	X	X	X
	- Lower Extremities			
Weakness				
Proximal	- Head/Neck	X	X	X
	- Shoulder	X	X	X
	- Trunk	X	X	X
Distal	- Upper Extremities	X	X	X
	- Lower Extremities			

Trumpet in normal playing position

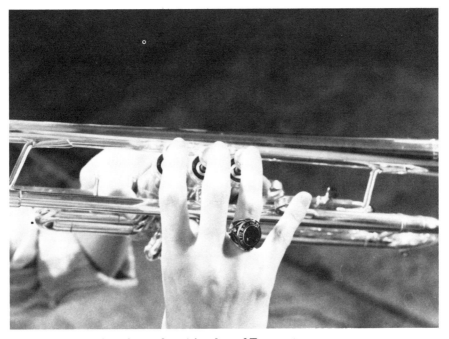

Right hand position (from above) in play of Trumpet

Left hand position in play of Trumpet

FAMILY: Brass
INSTRUMENT: Trumpet
TYPE: B-flat
MAKE AND MODEL: Olds Ambassador
MATERIALS: Brass

I. Assembly and Disassembly
The mouthpiece must be removed for transport or cleaning. This is accomplished by grasping the mouthpiece and pulling it from the instrument against resistance. A slight twisting movement may also be necessary.
NOTE: The mouthpiece is friction-fitted into the body of the instrument. If excessive pressure is applied, the mouthpiece will jam and should be removed with a special tool.

II. Tuning Requirements
The trumpet is tuned through the manipulation of tuning slides. These slides form an integral part of the instrument's tubing structure and are U-shaped. Action on these slides increases or diminishes the sounding length of the instrument. Slides are usually grasped with the thumb and first finger of the left hand and pushed or pulled against resistance.

III. Transport
The instrument is supplied with a hard shell case (plastic) which serves as a protective container and assists transport. Lighter weight, padded soft cases are also available.

IV. Student Maintenance
A. Tuning
The instrument must be tuned both before and during play.
B. Cleaning
1. Exterior surfaces must be wiped free of perspiration.
2. Interior surfaces
a. Interior of mouthpiece is cleaned with a bristle brush (mouthpiece brush), which is passed through.
b. Tuning slides are removed from body of instrument and cleaned by means of a bristle brush with a flexible shaft.
c. Interior of valve casing must be swabbed. This involves removal of the piston, which is located inside. Piston is removed by unscrewing a threaded disk located at the top of casings. A threaded disk located at bottom of each casing is also removed and the swab passed through.
3. The rest of the instrument is soaked in lukewarm water once pistons have been removed.
C. Water Keys
Saliva is invariably transmitted through the instrument during play and condensation forms within the bore. This situation affects both quality of tone and play-ability. Drainage is provided by the presence of keys located at the end of the two tuning slides near the bell of the instrument. The keys are depressed and accumulated moisture is shaken and blown from the instrument.
D. Lubrication
Tuning slides and the interior of the valve casings must be kept lightly oiled.

V. Variation Among Manufacturers
A. Mouthpieces
Mouthpieces are available from several sources and in many configurations. Diameter, length, weight, and interior dimensions vary. Stock sizes are available as well as custom-made mouthpieces. Selection of an appropriate size for student use is a musical as well as physical consideration.

B. Instrument

Dimensional variations among student grade instruments are negligible.

C. Cases

 1. A vinyl bag is available which will considerably diminish the transport weight and bulk. Bag is opened by a heavy zipper which runs along its length. Instrument protection is adequate unless dropped.

 2. Hard shell cases of wood composition may raise transport weight above 5 kg (11.02 lb.).

Instrument: Trumpet

Checklist

The following skills are necessary for independence in playing, owning, and receiving instruction on this instrument. The music teacher should confirm the need for those items, such as need for transport, which may not be necessary in all situations. The teacher should also add any items, such as the need to transport instructional materials to and from lessons, which may be applicable.

The therapist should indicate those requirements which a student is able to fulfill. The teacher or parents must provide for assistance in those areas in which a student may be dependent.

	Needed	Can Perform	Can Not Perform
1. Tune instrument			
2. Transport instrument			
3. Place instrument in case			
4. Open and close case			
5. Assemble instrument			
6. Disassemble instrument			
7. Clean instrument			
8. Apply lubricants			
9. Place instrument in playing position			
10. Operate water key			

TRUMPET (B-flat)

Considerations:
- General Body Position
- Major Body Parts Involved in Playing - Mobile/Stable Components - Functions of Major/Minor Joints Involved - Mobile/Stable Capacity

The trumpet is played in a manner requiring support *(stability)* and movement *(mobility)* of head/neck, trunk, and upper extremities. The major individual joints required to function in a stable capacity are those of the neck, shoulders, elbows, wrists, and left hand. Movement is of major importance in joints of the first three fingers of the right hand.

Considerations:
- Major Muscle Groups
- Movement Observed

The trumpet utilizes muscle groups to produce stabilization of the neck, shoulders, and elbows held in a flexed, abducted, and internally rotated fashion. Wrists are stable in extension (with ulnar deviation on the left) to hold instrument. Movement is produced in the first three digits of the right hand for finger flexion and extension.

Oral musculature produces lip closure and oral position for expelling wind. The degree of movement is greatest at metacarpophalangeal joints (MP) of the first three digits of the right hand.

Considerations:
- Muscle Strength
- Speed/Dexterity

Muscle strength utilized bilaterally in playing the trumpet requires holding the instrument up against gravity (Fair+ muscle grade) for periods of time. Additional strength is required for repetitive finger movements (Good- to Good muscle grade), increasing with playing time. The speed/dexterity of the right fingers relies on alternating up/down movements with isolated, coupled or mass digit execution, increasing with advanced playing.

Considerations:
- Sensation
- Perception

Playing the trumpet appears to utilize the deep sensations for positioning of arms and finger placement. Perceptual components appear to be in the areas of orientation and motor. Orientation mechanisms direct body movements in a planned coordinated fashion.

Considerations:
- Respiration
- Cardiac Output

The playing of the trumpet requires moderate exertion (light work), which may increase with prolonged playing.

Considerations:
- Vision
- Audition

The trumpet may be played by sighted individuals and also by those at any level of visual impairment. (Tactile/kinesthetic modalities may be primarily relied upon.) Auditory levels most functional are in the normal to moderate impairment range.

TRUMPET (B-flat)

MAJOR MUSCLE GROUPS USED IN PLAYING
WITHOUT SUBSTITUTION OR ADAPTATION

KEY: B=Beginning Level
      I =Intermediate Level
      A=Advanced Level

P=Held Position for Playing
X=Muscle Movement Used in Playing
•=Increased Usage

Body Part	Function	Muscle or Muscle Groups	Left B	Left I	Left A	Right B	Right I	Right A
Face Mouth		Mentalis	x	—	—	x	—	—
Scapula	Elevation	Trapezius (Inferior)	x	—	—	x	—	—
Shoulder	Flexion	Deltoideus (Anterior)	p	—	—	p	—	—
	Abduction	Deltoideus (Middle)	p	—	—	p	—	—
	Internal Rotation	Internal Rotator Group	p	—	—	p	—	—
Elbow	Flexion	Biceps Brachii Brachialis	p	—	—	p	—	—
Forearm	Pronation	Pronator Group	p	—	—	p	—	—
Wrist	Deviation, Ulnar	Flexor Carpi Ulnaris Extensor Carpi Ulnaris	p	—	—		—	—
	Extension	Extensor Carpi Rad. Longus & Brevis Extensor Carpi Ulnaris	p	—	—		—	—
	Flexion	Flexor Carpi Radial. Flexor Carpi Ulnaris	p	—	—	p	—	—

78

Body Part	Function	Muscle or Muscle Groups	Left B	Left I	Left A	Right B	Right I	Right A
Fingers	MP Flexion	Lumbricales	p	—	—	x	•	•
	IP Flexion (1st)	Flex. Digit. Superior	p	—	—	x	•	•
	IP Flexion (2nd)	Flex. Digit. Prof.	p	—	—	x	•	•
	MP Extension	Ext. Digit. Com.	—	—	—	x	•	•
	Adduction	Interossei Palmares	p	—	—	—	—	—
	Abduction	Interossei Dorsales	—	—	—	p	—	—
Thumb	IP Flexion	Flex. Poll. Longus	p	—	—	p	—	—
	Abduction	Abd. Poll. Brevis	—	—	—	—	—	—
	Abduction	Abd. Poll. Longus	p	—	—	p	—	—

Muscles listed are used in the playing of this instrument; those not listed are not directly involved.

Facial and neck musculature is marked on right and left for convenience.
Increases (•) are noted in Intermediate Level and Advanced Level that are most obvious.
Muscles are used in groups for synergist movements rather than as isolated muscle movements.
Generally, X's in Beginning Level continue in Intermediate and Advanced Levels.

TRUMPET (B-flat)

MOVEMENT OBSERVED IN PLAYING
(ACTIVE & POSITIONAL)
WITHOUT SUBSTITUTION OR ADAPTATION*

These ranges were determined through working with musicians. They reflect the musician's body size, individuality, and possibly style. The ranges are approximate to give a working baseline for instrument suitability.

Neck:		Neutral position.
Shoulders:		Flexed (50°), abducted (45°) and internally rotated (50°).
Elbows:		Flexed (90°) with abduction and internal rotation.
Forearms:	Left	Held in full pronation.
	Right	Held in full pronation.
Wrists:	Left	Extended (10°) and ulnar-deviated (30°).
	Right	Extended (40°).
Thumbs:	Left	IP flexed (60°) and abducted (40°).
	Right	Flexed and abducted around instrument.
Fingers:	Left	Flexed - MP (20°), PIP (90°), DIP (45°), with full ulnar deviation, and curled around instrument.
	Right	Flexed - MP (0-40°), PIP (60-100°), DIP (30-70°), 2nd, 3rd, 4th fingers. Fifth finger flexed - MP (70°), PIP (10°), DIP (10°), abducted (30°).

*I.e., using normal body position for playing, without any devices for instrument or body parts.

French Horn in normal playing position

Right hand position in play of French Horn

Left hand position in play of French Horn

FAMILY: Brass
INSTRUMENT: French Horn
MAKE AND MODEL: Conn 8D
MATERIALS USED IN CONSTRUCTION: Brass

I. Assembly and Disassembly
    The mouthpiece must be removed for transport or cleaning. This is accomplished by grasping the mouthpiece and pulling it from the instrument against resistance. A slight twisting movement may also be necessary.
    NOTE: The mouthpiece is friction-fitted into the body of the instrument. If excessive pressure is applied during assembly, the mouthpiece will jam and need to be removed with a special tool.

II. Tuning Requirements
    The French horn is tuned through the manipulation of nine tuning slides. These slides form an integral part of the instrument's tubing structure and are generally U-shaped. Action on these slides increases or diminishes the sounding length of the instrument. Slides are usually grasped with the thumb and first finger of the right hand and pushed or pulled against resistance.

III. Transport
    The instrument is supplied with a hard shell case (plastic) which serves as a protective container and assists transport.

IV. Student Maintenance
    A. Tuning
    The instrument must be tuned both before and during play.
    B. Cleaning
        1. Exterior surfaces must be wiped free of perspiration.
        2. Interior surfaces
            a. Interior of mouthpiece is cleaned with a bristle brush (mouthpiece brush), which is passed through.
            b. Body of instrument is cleaned by a brush or swab with a long, flexible shaft. Tuning slides must be removed for cleaning.
        3. Lubrication
        Tuning slides and valves must be kept lightly oiled.

V. Variation Among Manufacturers
    A. Instrument
    The instrument examined should not be considered a student-grade French horn. It is technically known as a double horn. This is due to the addition of the thumb-activated valve and additional tubing and slides. Addition of these keys enables the instrument to operate easily in the keys of F and B flat major. Some players report that the instrument is easier to play with the mechanical additions. The standard French horn is lighter, lacks the thumb-operated valve, and is considerably less expensive. Other dimensions are similar.
    B. Mouthpieces
    Mouthpieces are available from several sources and in many configurations. Diameter, length, weight, and interior dimensions vary. Stock sizes are available as well as custom-made mouthpieces. Selection of an appropriate size for student use is a musical as well as physical consideration.
    C. Cases
    Case weights may vary by as much as 1.5 kg (3.31 lb.).

Checklist

The following skills are necessary for independence in playing, owning, and receiving instruction on this instrument. The music teacher should confirm the need for those items, such as need for transport, which may not be necessary in all situations. The teacher should also add any items, such as the need to transport instructional materials to and from lessons, which may be applicable.

The therapist should indicate those requirements which a student is able to fulfill. The teacher or parents must provide for assistance in those areas in which a student may be dependent.

	Needed	Can Perform	Can Not Perform
1. Tune instrument	———	————	———
2. Transport instrument	———	————	———
3. Place instrument in case	———	————	———
4. Open and close case	———	————	———
5. Assemble instrument	———	————	———
6. Disassemble instrument	———	————	———
7. Clean instrument	———	————	———
8. Apply lubricants	———	————	———
9. Place instrument in playing position	———	————	———

FRENCH HORN

Considerations:
- General Body Position
- Major Body Parts Involved in Playing - Mobile/Stable Components - Functions of Major/Minor Joints Involved - Mobile/Stable Capacity

The French horn is played in a manner requiring support *(stability)* and movement *(mobility)* of head/neck, trunk, and upper extremities. The major individual joints required to function in a stable capacity are those of the neck, shoulders, elbows, wrists, and right hand. Movement is of major importance in the thumb and first three digits of the left hand.

Considerations:
- Major Muscle Groups
- Movement Observed

The French horn utilizes muscle groups to produce stabilization of the neck, shoulders, and elbows, to be held in a flexed, abducted, and internally rotated fashion. The right hand is supinated with fingers in a cone-shaped position (placed in bell of instrument). The left hand is pronated with the wrist stabilized in slight extension. Movements in the left hand are produced by flexion and extension. The oral musculature produces lip closure and oral positioning for expelling wind. The degree of movement is greatest in the proximal/interphalangeal (PIP) and the distal/interphalangeal (DIP) joints of the first three digits of the left hand and the metacarpophalangeal (MP) joints of the thumb.

Considerations:
- Muscle Strength
- Speed/Dexterity

Muscle strength utilized bilaterally in playing the French horn requires holding the left arm up against gravity; sufficient strength is needed to support the instrument for periods of time as it rests on lap (Fair+ to Good- muscle grade). Additional strength is required to depress keys, increasing with playing time (Good- to Good muscle grade). Spring tension of keys can be altered to increase or decrease resistance. The speed/dexterity of the left fingers relies on alternating upward/downward movements with isolated, coupled or mass digit execution.

Considerations:
- Sensation
- Perception

Playing the French horn appears to utilize the deep sensations for positioning of arms and finger placement. Perceptual components appear to be in the areas of orientation and motor. Orientation mechanisms direct body movements in a planned, coordinated manner.

Considerations:
- Respiration
- Cardiac Output

The playing of the French horn requires moderate exertion (light work), which may increase with prolonged playing.

Considerations:
- Vision
- Audition

The French horn may be played by sighted individuals and also by those at any level of visual impairment. (Tactile/kinesthetic modalities may be primarily relied upon.) Auditory levels most functional are in the normal to moderate impairment range.

FRENCH HORN

MAJOR MUSCLE GROUPS USED IN PLAYING
WITHOUT SUBSTITUTION OR ADAPTATION

KEY: B=Beginning Level I =Intermediate Level A=Advanced Level

P=Held Position for Playing
X=Muscle Movement Used in Playing
•=Increased Usage

Body Part	Function	Muscle or Muscle Groups	Left B	Left I	Left A	Right B	Right I	Right A
Face Mouth		Mentalis	x	—	—	x	—	—
Neck	Flexion & Rotation	Sternocleidomastoideus	p	—	—	p	—	—
Scapula	Elevation	Trapezius (Inferior)	x	—	—	x	—	—
Shoulder	Flexion	Deltoideus (Anterior)	p	—	—		—	—
	Internal Rotation	Internal Rotator Group	p	—	—	p	—	—
Elbow	Flexion	Biceps Brachii Brachialis	p	—	—	p	—	—
Forearm	Supination	Supinator Group		—	—		—	—
	Pronation	Pronator Group	p	—	—	p	—	—
Wrist	Extension	Extensor Carpi Ulnaris	p	—	—	p	—	—
	Flexion	Flexor Carpi Radial. Flexor Carpi Ulnaris	p	—	—	p	—	—

Body Part	Function	Muscle or Muscle Groups	B	Left I	Left A	Right B	Right I	Right A
Fingers	MP Flexion	Lumbricales	x			p		
	IP Flexion (1st)	Flex. Digit. Superior	x			p		
	IP Flexion (2nd)	Flex. Digit. Prof.	x			p		
	MP Extension	Ext. Digit. Com.	x			p		
	Adduction	Interossei Palmares						
	Abduction	Interossei Dorsales	p*			p		
	Opposition	Opponens Digit. Min.				p		
Thumb	MP Flexion	Flex. Poll. Brevis	x					
	IP Flexion	Flex. Poll. Longus	x					
	MP Extension	Ext. Poll. Brevis	x					
	IP Extension	Ext. Poll. Longus	x					
	Abduction	Abd. Poll. Brevis						
		Abd. Poll. Longus						
	Adduction	Add. Poll.	x			p		

*Fifth finger only

Muscles listed are used in the playing of this instrument; those not listed are not directly involved.

Facial and neck musculature is marked on right and left for convenience.
Increases (•) are noted in Intermediate Level and Advanced Level that are most obvious.
Muscles are used in groups for synergist movements rather than as isolated muscle movements.
Generally, X's in Beginning Level continue in Intermediate and Advanced Levels.

FRENCH HORN

MOVEMENT OBSERVED IN PLAYING
(ACTIVE & POSITIONAL)
WITHOUT SUBSTITUTION OR ADAPTATION*

These ranges were determined through working with musicians. They reflect the musician's body size, individuality, and possibly style. The ranges are approximate to give a working baseline for instrument suitability.

Neck:		Rotated (10°) to left shoulder.
Shoulders:	Left	Flexed (20°), internally rotated (40°).
	Right	Held at neutral (at side) with internal rotation (30°).
Elbows:	Left	Flexed (110°).
	Right	Flexed (90°).
Forearms:	Left	Pronated (20°).
	Right	Supinated (10°).
Wrists:	Left	Extended (30°).
	Right	Extended (20°).
Thumbs:	Left	Abducted (60°) with and flexes at MP (0-30°).
	Right	Adducted to index finger in cone shape.
Fingers:	Left	(2,3,4) flexes MP (10-20°), PIP (60-90°), DIP (40-55°). (5th) MP - neutral, PIP (60°), DIP (55°), and abducted on finger rest.
	Right	Held in cone-shaped position.

*I.e., using normal body position for playing, without any devices for instrument or body parts.

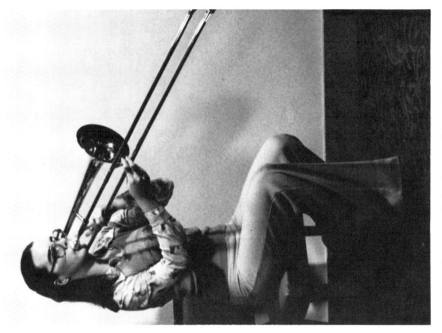

Trombone in normal playing position (slide mid-way)

Trombone in normal playing position (slide extended)

89

Hand positions in play of Trombone (top view)

Right hand position in play of Trombone

FAMILY: Brass
INSTRUMENT: Trombone
TYPE: Slide
MAKE: King
MODEL: Cleveland 605
MATERIALS USED IN CONSTRUCTION: Brass

I. Assembly and Disassembly
    A. Mechanical Attachments
       1. The mouthpiece is friction-fitted to the slide assembly with metal-to-metal contact and must be removed for transport or cleaning. This is accomplished by grasping the mouthpiece and pulling it from the assembly against some resistance. A slight twisting motion may also be necessary.
       NOTE: If excessive pressure is applied during assembly the mouthpiece may jam and need to be removed with a special tool.
       2. The slide and bell assemblies are joined by a threaded socket joint with a sliding sleeve. This arrangement is similar to the type of coupling used to join a garden hose to a faucet. One hand must hold the pieces together while the other hand tightens the sleeve.
       3. The slide must be locked in place during assembly and disassembly. This is accomplished by a clip located at the end of the slide near the mouthpiece. When a ring located at the end of the slide is turned, the clip engages a catch located on the adjacent piece.
    B. Alignment of Pieces
       Pieces must be spaced so that adequate clearance is maintained between the player's hand and the bell. Care must also be taken to insure that the location of the bars used for prehension allows for instrument support. Arrangement of pieces is accomplished through visual sighting and adjustment of the threaded coupling.

II. Tuning Requirements
    The trombone is tuned by adjustment of a tuning slide located behind the bell of the instrument. Action on this slide increases or diminishes the sounding level of the instrument. It must be pushed or pulled against some resistance.

III. Transport
    1. The instrument is supplied with a hard shell (plastic) case which serves as a protective container and assists transport. Disassembly is required.
    2. Case interior
       The bell assembly of the instrument is located in the lower portion of the case and the slide assembly is retained in the lid. Each is kept in its place by plastic strips which pivot on a screw. These keepers are rotated to release or retain each part. The mouthpiece is located in a separate compartment within the case.

IV. Student Maintenance
    A. The instrument must be tuned both before and during play.
    B. Cleaning
       1. Exterior surfaces must be wiped clean of perspiration.
       2. Interior surfaces
          a. Interior of mouthpiece is cleaned with a bristle brush, which is passed through.
          b. Remainder of instrument is disassembled and cleaned with a brush or swab with a long, flexible shaft.
    C. Water key (spit valve)
       Saliva is invariably transmitted through the instrument and condensation forms within the bore. This situation affects both quality of tone and playability. Drainage is provided by a key located at the end of the playing slide. This key is depressed and the accumulated moisture is shaken from the instrument.

D. Lubrication
Both the tuning slide and the playing slide must be kept well-lubricated with special oils. This procedure is critical in the case of the playing (long) slide because of its almost constant movement during play.

V. Variation Among Manufacturers
A. Student-model trombones are without great dimensional variation; however, there are several options or additions available at additional expense which may be worth considering. The F attachment is an additional length of tubing which is engaged by a valve. This attachment extends the effective playing range of the instrument. Valve assemblies are available which replace the slide on the instrument with a mechanism similar to that found on a trumpet. The sound is similar to that of a trombone, but slide movement is eliminated.
B. Mouthpieces
Mouthpieces are available from several sources and in many configurations. Diameter, length, weight and interior dimensions vary. Stock sizes are available as well as custom-made mouthpieces. Selection of an appropriate size for student use is a musical as well as physical consideration.

Instrument: Trombone

Checklist

The following skills are necessary for independence in playing, owning, and receiving instruction on this instrument. The music teacher should confirm the need for those items, such as need for transport, which may not be necessary in all situations. The teacher should also add any items, such as the need to transport instructional materials to and from lessons, which may be applicable.

The therapist should indicate those requirements which a student is able to fulfill. The teacher or parents must provide for assistance in those areas in which a student may be dependent.

	Needed	Can Perform	Can Not Perform
1. Tune instrument	___	___	___
2. Transport instrument	___	___	___
3. Place instrument in case	___	___	___
4. Open and close case	___	___	___
5. Assemble instrument	___	___	___
6. Disassemble instrument	___	___	___
7. Clean instrument	___	___	___
8. Apply lubricants	___	___	___
9. Place instrument in playing position	___	___	___
10. Operate water key	___	___	___
10. Operate slide lock	___	___	___

TROMBONE (With F Attachment)

Considerations:
- General Body Position
- Major Body Parts Involved in Playing - Mobile/Stable Components - Functions of Major/Minor Joints Involved - Mobile/Stable Capacity

The trombone is played in a manner requiring support *(stability)* and movement *(mobility)* of head/neck, trunk, and upper extremities. The major individual joints required to function in a stable capacity are those of the neck, left shoulder, left elbow, wrists, fingers, and right hand. Movement is of major importance in the right shoulder, right elbow, right wrist, and left thumb (F attachment).

Considerations:
- Major Muscle Groups
- Movement Observed

Playing the trombone utilizes muscle groups to produce neck stability and stability of the left shoulder, elbow and wrist in a flexed, externally rotated and pronated position. Flexion, extension, abduction, and rotation are produced in the right upper extremity. The right hand movements include extension and deviation. Oral musculature produces lip closure and oral positioning for expelling wind. Movement is greatest for the right elbow, right wrist, and the index and middle fingers of the right hand. Movement is utilized to a lesser degree in the right shoulder and the left thumb (F attachment).

Considerations:
- Muscle Strength
- Speed/Dexterity

Muscle strength utilized bilaterally in playing the trombone requires holding the instrument up against gravity; (Fair+ to Good- muscle grade) for periods of time. Additional strength is required for right upper extremity moving in/out of positions (Good- to Good muscle grade), increasing with playing time. The speed/dexterity of playing the trombone is a gross motor function requiring skilled, fine motor planning from position to position.

Considerations:
- Sensation
- Perception

Playing the trombone appears to utilize the deep sensations for arm movements. Perceptual components appear to be in the areas of orientation, visual, and motor. (Exclude visual for non-sighted individuals.) Orientation mechanisms direct body movement using visual cues in a planned, coordinated manner.

Considerations:
- Respiration
- Cardiac Output

The playing of the trombone requires moderate exertion (light work), which may increase with prolonged playing.

Considerations:
- Vision
- Audition

The trombone may be played by sighted individuals and also by those at any level of visual impairment. (Tactile/kinesthetic modalities may be primarily relied upon.) Auditory levels most functional are in the normal to moderate impairment range.

TROMBONE (With F Attachment)

MAJOR MUSCLE GROUPS USED IN PLAYING
WITHOUT SUBSTITUTION OR ADAPTATION

KEY: B=Beginning Level   P=Held Position for Playing
         I =Intermediate Level   X=Muscle Movement Used in Playing
         A=Advanced Level   •=Increased Usage

Body Part	Function	Muscle or Muscle Groups	Left B	Left I	Left A	Right B	Right I	Right A
Face Mouth		Mentalis	x	—	—	x	—	—
Scapula	Elevation	Trapezius (Inferior)	x	—	—	x	—	—
Shoulder	Flexion	Deltoideus (Anterior)	p	—	—	x	—	—
	Abduction	Deltoideus (Middle)	p	—	—	x	—	—
	External Rotation	External Rotator Group				x	—	—
	Internal Rotation	Internal Rotator Group	p	—	—	x	—	—
Elbow	Flexion	Biceps Brachii						
		Brachialis	p	—	—	x	—	—
Forearm	Supination	Supinator Group				x	—	—
	Pronation	Pronator Group	p	—	—	x	—	—
Wrist	Deviation, Radial	Flexor Carpi Radial.						
		Extensor Carpi Rad. Longus				x		—
		Extensor Carpi Rad. Brevis						
	Deviation, Ulnar	Flexor Carpi Ulnaris				x		—
	Extension	Extensor Carpi Ulnaris						
		Extensor Carpi Rad. Longus & Brevis	p	—	—	x	—	—
	Flexion	Flexor Carpi Radial.	p	—	—	x	—	—
		Flexor Carpi ...				x		

Body Part	Function	Muscle or Muscle Groups	Left			Right		
			B	I	A	B	I	A
Fingers	MP Flexion	Lumbricales	p	—	—	—	x	—
	IP Flexion (1st)	Flex. Digit. Superior	p	—	—	—	x	—
	IP Flexion (2nd)	Flex. Digit. Prof.	p	—	—	—	x	—
	MP Extension	Ext. Digit. Com.	—	—	—	—	x	—
	Adduction	Interossei Palmares	p	—	—	—	p	—
	Abduction	Abduct. Digit. Min.	—	—	—	—	p	—
Thumb	MP Flexion	Flex. Poll. Brevis*	x	•	—	—	x	—
	IP Flexion	Flex. Poll. Longus*	x	•	—	—	x	—
	Abduction	Abd. Poll. Brevis	—	—	—	—	—	—
		Abd. Poll. Longus	p	—	—	—	p	—

*F-Attachment

Muscles listed are used in the playing of this instrument; those not listed are not directly involved.

Facial and neck musculature is marked on right and left for convenience.
Increases (•) are noted in Intermediate Level and Advanced Level that are most obvious.
Muscles are used in groups for synergist movements rather than as isolated muscle movements.
Generally, X's in Beginning Level continue in Intermediate and Advanced Levels.

TROMBONE (With F Attachment)

MOVEMENT OBSERVED IN PLAYING
(ACTIVE & POSITIONAL)
WITHOUT SUBSTITUTION OR ADAPTATION*

These ranges were determined through working with musicians. They reflect the musician's body size, individuality, and possibly style. The ranges are approximate to give a working baseline for instrument suitability.

Head:		Neutral position.
Shoulders:	Left	Flexed (40°), abducted (30°), with internal rotation (60°).
	Right	Flexes (40–60°), abducted (40–50°) with internal rotation (30–60°), increasing as hand moves toward mouth.
Elbows:	Left	Flexed (120°) with shoulder abduction and rotation.
	Right	Flexes (0–130°) with shoulder abduction and rotation.
Forearms:	Left	Pronated (20°) in a holding position.
	Right	Pronates (0–40°).
Wrists:	Left	Held in neutral position.
	Right	Extends (0–30°) with ulnar deviation (0–20°), increasing as hand moves away from mouth.
Thumbs:	Left	Abducted (40°) and flexes (0–30°) when F attachment is used.
	Right	Positioned in abduction against slide bar opposite index finger.
Fingers:	Left	Held in flexion around instrument except index, which is partially extended for stabilization against mouthpiece. MP - (30°) flexion, index finger MP - (40°) flexion, 3, 4, 5 fingers PIP - (0°) flexion, index finger PIP - (60°) flexion, 3, 4, 5 fingers DIP - (0°) flexion, index finger DIP - (40°) flexion, 3, 4, 5 fingers
	Right	Flexes (0–60°) at knuckle joints, increasing as hand moves toward mouth. Index finger and 3rd fully extended under slide bar with 4th, 5th positioned in fist fashion.

*I.e., using normal body position for playing, without any devices for instrument or body parts.

96

FAMILY: WOODWIND

INSTRUMENTS: B-Flat CLARINET

FLUTE

SAXOPHONE (Alto & Tenor)

RECORDER (Soprano & Alto)

INTRODUCTION

The saxophone and clarinet produce sound by a reed, a thin piece of wood or plastic, that vibrates when pressure is applied and an airstream provided. The result of applying facial muscle pressure, or tension, for the purpose of directing an airstream by the musician to the sound-producing agent of an instrument, is called the embouchure. All the woodwinds are essentially resonating tubes which act upon the sound produced by an agent (in the case of the clarinet and saxophone, a reed) which has already reacted to the embouchure, and wind pressures produced by the player.

The flute player (or flutist) induces the instrument to sound by directing an airstream toward an open hole called the embouchure hole. This hole literally splits the airstream and thus produces sound. This process is often compared to blowing into a soda bottle to produce sound.

The recorder comes with a ready made embouchure. The airstream is directed through a passage which leads to a tapered edge of wood or plastic, and splits the "guided airstream" to produce sound. The recorder is the only woodwind with such a passage, and it is also the only family member which lacks the amazing assortment of keys, rods, levers, springs, and posts that are the hallmark of its relatives.

Varying the length of a resonating tube results in variation in the pitch of the tone produced. Boring a hole in the side of a resonating tube effectively shortens its sounding length. Boring many holes along its length permits the single tube to take on the characteristics of many shorter ones, provided the then unneeded holes can be sealed. The holes in a recorder can be covered by unassisted fingers and need no keys (at least on the soprano and alto), but the number of holes that can be placed on a tube and the distances between them for the production of different sounds exceed the ability and efficiency of the human hand.

The evolution of keys has taken place over hundreds of years and has been influenced by physics, acoustics, mechanics, the needs of musicians, the desire of composers, and the genius of instrument makers, but for many centuries they have been a musical embodiment of man's desire to overcome his physical limitations in the production of sound.

THE WOODWIND INSTRUMENTS
SPECIAL CONSIDERATIONS

I. SINGLE REED INSTRUMENTS

Instruments: Listed in order of increased size of reed, mouthpiece, and instrument:
Clarinet E-flat Soprano & B-flat
Saxophone E-flat Alto & B-flat Tenor

Considerations: • Embouchure

The lower lip is drawn slightly over the lower teeth and about one-half of the mouthpiece is placed between the lips. The reed rests against the lower lip with the upper teeth upon the mouthpiece. The lips are drawn back or closed firmly around the mouthpiece so that no air escapes. The lower jaw is positioned downward and slightly forward.

Considerations: • Facial Muscles Involved

The muscles involved in order of importance are the orbicularis oris, triangularis, quadratus labii inferioris, platysma, supra- and infrahyoid groups, buccinator, and risorius.

Considerations: • Dental Occlusion
                        • Dental Irregularities

Instruments are contraindicated if the individual has the following occlusions:

Class I with protruding upper anterior teeth
All Class II, Division 1 and 2
Some Class III

The following dental irregularities may contraindicate the playing of these instruments:

Anterior crossbite and crowding and/or rotation
Extreme anterior spacing of the maxillary and mandibular incisors.

Considerations: • Respiration

Normal vital capacity is recommended. The preferred method of breathing is diaphragmatic. The pattern of breathing is rapid inspirations followed by prolonged and discontinuous expirations.

II. DOUBLE REED INSTRUMENTS

Instruments: Oboe
Bassoon

Note: Neither the oboe or bassoon have been included in the main body of the text as they are considered to be more than usually difficult for beginning students. This should not preclude them from consideration in all cases, however, and we therefore include the following.

Considerations: • Embouchure

Both lips are drawn slightly inward to cover the teeth during adjustment to the double reed. About one-eighth to one-quarter of the reed is placed in the mouth and rests firmly on the lower lip. Both lips are then closed to prevent air escape. The teeth support the lips and the mandible moves slightly downward and forward during adjustment.

Considerations: • Facial Muscles Involved

The buccinator, orbicularis oris, caninus, and triangularis are the most important muscles used in playing.

Considerations: • Dental Occlusion
                    • Dental Irregularities

Instruments are contraindicated if the individual has a complicated Class I occlusion. Anterior crossbite and crowding and/or rotation may affect embouchure formation.

Considerations: • Respiration

Normal vital capacity is recommended. The preferred method of breathing is diaphragmatic. The pattern of breathing is the same for the Class B and Class D instruments except for the oboe where there is low expiratory flow rate.

III. FLUTES

These instruments have a hole or aperture in the head of the instrument for a mouthpiece.

Instruments: Flute C & E-flat

Considerations: • Embouchure

The lower lip is rolled over the side of the head of the instrument so that the edge forms a straight line across the hole. The upper lip is stretched downward to form a small aperture. There is less precision in jaw movement and the tones are produced by increasing or lessening the tension of the upper lip.

Considerations: • Facial Muscles Involved

The muscles of most importance are the orbicularis oris, triangularis, and risorius.

Considerations: • Dental Occlusion
                    • Dental Irregularities

Instruments are contraindicated if the individual has the following occlusions:

> Class II, Divisions 1 and 2
> Complicated Class I
> Some Class III

Anterior crossbite and crowding and/or rotation may affect embouchure formation.

Considerations: • Respiration

Normal vital capacity is recommended. The preferred method of breathing is diaphragmatic. The pattern of breathing is rapid inspirations followed by prolonged and discontinuous expirations.

INSTRUMENT SELECTION GUIDE

An "X" indicates a potential physical limitation in relationship to "normal" use of the instrument. The presence of an "X" should not necessarily preclude consideration of the instrument if compensatory techniques and adaptations are appropriate.

Potential Limitations	B-flat Clarinet	Flute	Saxophone (A/T)	Recorder (S/A)
Contractures of				
Neck				
Shoulders	X	X	X	X
Elbows	X	X	X	X
Wrists	X	X	X	X
Fingers	X	X	X	X
Hips	X	X	X	X
Knees				
Ankles				
Incoordination				
Gross - Upper Extremities				
- Lower Extremities				
Fine - Upper Extremities	X	X	X	X
- Lower Extremities				
Limb Loss (prosthesis fit implied)				
- Upper Extremities				
- Above Elbow	X	X	X	X
- Below Elbow	X	X	X	X
- Partial Hand	X	X	X	X
- Lower Extremities				
- Above Knee				
- Below Knee				
- Symes				
- Partial Foot				
- Hip Disarticulation				

Potential Limitations	B-flat Clarinet	Flute	Saxophone (A/T)	Recorder (S/A)
Movement				
Athetoid - Upper Extremities	X	X	X	X
- Lower Extremities				
Rigidity - Upper Extremities	X	X	X	X
- Lower Extremities				
Fluctuating Tone				
- Upper Extremities	X	X	X	X
- Lower Extremities				
Tremor				
Resting - Upper Extremities	X	X	X	X
Intention - Upper Extremities	X	X	X	X
- Upper Extremities	X	X	X	X
Dysmetria				
Pain	X	X	X	X
Perception - Children				
Apraxia	X	X	∧	X
Posture & Bilateral Integration	X	X	X	X
Space Visual	X			
- Adult				
Neglect	X	X	X	X
Hemianopsia	X	X	X	X
Spatial	X	X	X	X
Apraxia	X	X	X	X
Sensation				
Tactile	X	X	X	X
Proprioception	X	X	X	X
Kinesthesia	X	X	X	X

Potential Limitations	B-flat Clarinet	Flute	Saxophone (A/T)	Recorder (S/A)
Spasticity - Upper Extremities	X	X	X	X
- Lower Extremities				
Weakness				
Proximal - Head/Neck	X	X	X	X
- Shoulder	X	X	X	X
- Trunk	X	X	X	X
Distal - Upper Extremities	X	X	X	X
- Lower Extremities				

Clarinet in normal playing position

Hand positions in play of Clarinet

FAMILY: Woodwind
INSTRUMENT: Clarinet
TYPE: B-flat
MAKE: Yamaha
MODEL: YCL 24
MATERIALS USED IN CONSTRUCTION: Plastic

I. Assembly and Disassembly
   A. Mechanical attachment
      1. Joints are friction-fitted with plastic to lubricated cork surface.
      2. Reed is held to mouthpiece through the use of a circular clamp called the ligature.
   B. Method of disassembly
      1. Adjacent pieces are grasped and pulled apart with a twisting motion against some resistance. Care must be taken to avoid damaging the key mechanisms.
      2. Reed is removed by loosening of ligature *(see Student Maintenance)*.
   C. Method of assembly
      1. Adjacent pieces are grasped and pushed together with a twisting motion against some resistance. Care must be taken to avoid damage to key mechanisms.
      2. See *Student Maintenance* for reed assembly.
   D. Alignment of pieces
      The clarinet is aligned through visual sighting of various keys and pieces in relation to one another. Adjacent pieces are grasped and twisted against some resistance. Care must be taken to avoid damaging key mechanisms. Two hands are needed to perform this operation.

II. Tuning Requirements
    The clarinet is tuned by grasping the mouthpiece and adjacent piece and pulling them apart, or pushing them together, with a twisting motion against some resistance. Alignment of pieces must be maintained and care must be taken to avoid damaging key mechanisms.

III. Transport
     The instrument is supplied with a hard shell (vinyl over fiber case), which serves as a protective container during transport. Disassembly is required.

IV. Student Maintenance
    A. Tuning
       The instrument must be tuned both before and during play.
    B. Cleaning
       1. The instrument should be cleaned (wipe interior) after playing.
       2. Devices used are swab, and swab on string.
          a. Swab is essentially a stick with absorbent material at one end. It is passed through disassembled pieces.
          b. Swab on string is a weighted string which is attached to a cloth and is dropped through the disassembled instrument. The cloth is then drawn through.
    C. Lubrication
       Cork joints must be periodically lubricated with a grease or waxlike substance. Lubricant is taken from a small container and spread over cork.
    D. Reed replacement
       The reed is a piece of material, usually cane, which is the sound-producing agent of the instrument. It is fragile and usually protected by a metal sheath which is placed over the mouthpiece when the instrument is idle. Reeds must be routinely replaced, often during play, and this requires the loosening of two small thumbscrews (8 mm x 10 mm) which secure the ligature and reed to the mouthpiece. Replacement requires fine alignment of the new reed in relation to the mouthpiece with simultaneous tightening of the ligature.

The clarinet is a sophisticated mechanical device which requires the adjustment of rods, levers, and springs from time to time as well as replacement of parts such as key pads (found on the underside of keys and used to seal the opening between key and body of instrument) which are subject to deterioration. This work is referred to a highly skilled repair person and should be performed on a routine basis.

V. Variation Among Manufacturers
  A. Materials and dimensions
     Clarinets are also made of wood, which is the material of choice for more expensive instruments. Dimensions do not vary significantly among the student grade instruments, nor are options such as additional or offset keys available without considerable increases in price.
  B. Reeds and mouthpieces
     Both items are available in various sizes and grades. Outside dimensions, however, are similar. Players report variation in breath pressures needed to play when using various combinations. Selection of appropriate mouthpieces and reeds is a musical as well as physical consideration.

Instrument: B-flat Clarinet

Checklist

The following skills are necessary for independence in playing, owning, and receiving instruction on this instrument. The music teacher should confirm the need for those items, such as need for transport, which may not be necessary in all situations. The teacher should also add any items, such as the need to transport instructional materials to and from lessons, which may be applicable.

The therapist should indicate those requirements which a student is able to fulfill. The teacher or parents must provide for assistance in those areas in which a student may be dependent.

	Needed	Can Perform	Can Not Perform
1. Tune instrument			
2. Transport instrument			
3. Place instrument in case			
4. Open and close case			
5. Assemble instrument			
6. Disassemble instrument			
7. Clean instrument			
8. Apply lubricants			
9. Place instrument in playing position			
10. Align pieces			
11. Replace reeds			

CLARINET (B-flat)

Considerations:
- General Body Position
- Major Body Parts Involved in Playing - Mobile/Stable Components - Functions of Major/Minor Joints Involved - Mobile/Stable Capacity

The clarinet is played in a manner requiring support *(stability)* and movement *(mobility)* of head/neck, trunk, and upper extremities. The major individual joints required to function in a stable capacity are those of the neck, shoulders, elbows, and wrists bilaterally, used in a stable capacity. Movement is of major importance in joints of the fingers bilaterally.

Considerations:
- Major Muscle Groups
- Movement Observed

The clarinet utilizes muscle groups to produce stabilization of shoulders, elbows, and wrist. The position assumed is one in which the shoulders are flexed, abducted, and internally rotated, the elbows flexed and the wrists pronated. Wrists are stabilized in slight extension with primary movements of flexion, extension, abduction, and adduction produced in the fingers. Oral musculature produces lip closure and oral positioning for expelling wind. The degree of movement is shared at the MP and IP joints of the hands bilaterally.

Considerations:
- Muscle Strength
- Speed/Dexterity

Muscle strength utilized bilaterally in playing the clarinet requires holding the instrument up against gravity (Fair+ to Good muscle grade) for periods of time. Additional strength is required to cover and uncover opening and to press keys (Good- to Good muscle grade), increasing with playing time. The speed/dexterity of the fingers relies on rolling, alternating upward/downward movements with isolated, coupled, and mass finger execution. Demands increase with advanced playing.

Considerations:
- Sensation
- Perception

Playing the clarinet appears to utilize the deep sensations for positioning arms and finger placement. Perceptual components appear to be in the areas of orientation and motor. Orientation mechanisms direct body movements in a planned, coordinated manner.

Considerations:
- Respiration
- Cardiac Output

The playing of the clarinet requires moderate exertion (light work), which may increase with prolonged playing.

Considerations:
- Vision
- Audition

The clarinet may be played by sighted individuals and also by those at any level of visual impairment. (Tactile/kinesthetic modalities may be primarily relied upon.) Auditory levels most functional are in the normal to moderate impairment range.

CLARINET (B-flat)

MAJOR MUSCLE GROUPS USED IN PLAYING
WITHOUT SUBSTITUTION OR ADAPTATION

KEY: B=Beginning Level
I =Intermediate Level
A=Advanced Level

P=Held Position for Playing
X=Muscle Movement Used in Playing
•=Increased Usage

Body Part	Function	Muscle or Muscle Groups	Left			Right		
			B	I	A	B	I	A
Face Mouth		Mentalis	x			x		
Scapula	Elevation	Trapezius (Inferior)	x			x		
Shoulder	Flexion	Deltoideus (Anterior)	p			p		
	Abduction	Deltoideus (Middle)	p			p		
	Internal Rotation	Internal Rotator Group	p			p		
Elbow	Flexion	Biceps Brachii Brachialis	p			p		
Forearm	Supination	Supinator Group		x	•			
	Pronation	Pronator Group	p	x	•	p		
Wrist	Deviation, Radial	Flexor Carpi Radial.	p					
		Extensor Carpi Rad. Longus	p	x	•			
	Extension	Extensor Carpi Ulnaris	p			p		
	Flexion	Flexor Carpi Radial.				p		
		Flexor Carpi Ulnaris	p			p		

Body Part	Function	Muscle or Muscle Groups	Left B	Left I	Left A	Right B	Right I	Right A
Fingers	MP Flexion	Lumbricales	x			x		
	IP Flexion (1st)	Flex. Digit. Superior	x			x		
	IP Flexion (2nd)	Flex. Digit. Prof.	x			x		
	MP Extension	Ext. Digit. Com.	x			x		
	Adduction	Interossei Palmares	x			x		
	Abduction	Interossei Dorsales	x			x		
		Abduct. Digit. Min.				x		
Thumb	MP Flexion	Flex. Poll. Brevis	x					
	Abduction	Abd. Poll. Brevis				p		
		Abd. Poll. Longus	x					
	Adduction	Add. Poll.	x					

Muscles listed are used in the playing of this instrument; those not listed are not directly involved.

Facial and neck musculature is marked on right and left for convenience.
Increases (•) are noted in Intermediate Level and Advanced Level that are most obvious.
Muscles are used in groups for synergist movements rather than as isolated muscle movements.
Generally, X's in Beginning Level continue in Intermediate and Advanced Levels.

CLARINET (B-flat)

MOVEMENT OBSERVED IN PLAYING
(ACTIVE & POSITIONAL)
WITHOUT SUBSTITUTION OR ADAPTATION*

These ranges were determined through working with musicians. They reflect the musician's body size, individuality, and possibly style. The ranges are approximate to give a working baseline for instrument suitability.

Head:		Neutral
Shoulders:		Neutral (at sides) with slight abduction (10°), and internally rotated (50°).
Elbows:	Left	Flexed (100°).
	Right	Flexed (90°).
Forearms:	Left	Pronated (30°).
	Right	Pronated (40°).
Wrists:	Left	Extended (30°) with slight radial deviation during play.
	Right	Extended (20°).
Thumbs:	Left	Abducted (60°) and flexes (0–30°).
	Right	Abducted (50°).
Fingers:		Flexes MP (20–40°), PIP (30–60°), DIP (10–30°) with some adjustments of abduction and adduction especially of the fifth fingers.

*I.e., using normal body position for playing, without any devices for instrument or body parts.

Flute in normal playing position

Flute in normal playing position (close view)

Hand positions in play of Flute (top view over player's shoulder)

Hand positions in play of Flute (Front view)

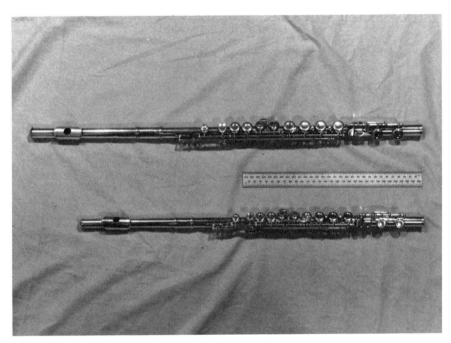

Comparison of Flute in C (top) to Small Flute (bottom)

FAMILY: Woodwind
INSTRUMENT: Flute
TYPES: C and E-flat
MAKE: Yamaha   Armstrong
MODEL: Yfl 24N C   2-4460 E-flat
MATERIALS USED IN CONSTRUCTION: Metal

Note: The E-flat flute is not a student-grade instrument and may be difficult to obtain. It is included because its smaller size may make it desirable. Players report increased air volume is needed to play the E-flat flute.

I.   Assembly and Disassembly
   A.   Mechanical attachment
   Joints are friction-fitted with metal to metal contact.
   B.   Method of disassembly
   Adjacent pieces are grasped and pulled apart with a twisting motion against some resistance. Care must be taken to avoid damaging key mechanisms.
   C.   Method of assembly
   Adjacent pieces are grasped and pushed together with a twisting motion against some resistance. Care must be taken to avoid damaging key mechanisms.
   D.   Alignment of pieces
      1.   C Flute
      Alignment marks are provided.
      2.   E-flat Flute
      Instrument is aligned through visual sighting of various keys and pieces in relation to one another.
   On both instruments the player grasps adjacent pieces and twists them against some resistance. Care must be taken to avoid damaging key mechanisms. Two hands are needed for this operation.

II.   Tuning Requirements
   The flute is tuned by grasping the mouthpiece and barrel and pulling them apart, or pushing them together, with a twisting motion against some resistance. Alignment of pieces must be maintained, and care must be taken to avoid damaging key mechanisms.

III.   Transport
   The instruments are supplied with a hard shell (plastic, C-flute; wood composition, E-flat flute) case, which serves as a protective container during transport. Disassembly is required.

IV.   Student Maintenance
   A.   Tuning
   The instrument must be tuned both before and during play.
   B.   Cleaning
      1.   The instrument should be cleaned (wipe interior) after playing.
      2.   Device used-swab. The swab is a stick with absorbent material placed at one end. It is passed through each length of the disassembled instrument.
   C.   Lubrication
   Key mechanisms and joints must be lightly lubricated from time to time.

The flute is a sophisticated mechanical device which requires the adjustment of rods, levers, and springs from time to time, as well as replacement of parts such as key pads (found on the underside of keys and used to seal the opening between key and body of instrument) which are subject to deterioration. This work is referred to a highly skilled repair person and should be performed on a routine basis.

V. Variation Among Manufacturers
  A. Dimensional variations among student-grade flutes are not significant; however, there are options available on these instruments which may add or detract from the appropriateness of a given model for use.
    1. Offset G Key (E-flat flute examined has this feature.)
       A flute with this feature has a key moved somewhat closer to the fourth finger of the left hand. Overall hand position may be altered.
    2. Additional Key on Footjoint
       The footjoint may be extended for the addition of a key which, when depressed will sound the note B. This would be played by the fifth finger on the right hand.
    3. Open-holed
       Flutes referred to as being "open-holed" have some of the keys perforated. Players report that this allows for a better tone. The student must depress the key and maintain a seal over the perforation with their finger.
  B. Extensive variations within the key mechanisms and embouchure plate of the instrument are available on more expensive models. The appropriateness of these modifications is a question of individual needs. Questions regarding the extension of, addition to, any mechanisms should be referred to a skilled repair person and teacher to determine feasibility and expense.

Instrument: Flute (C or E-flat)

Checklist

The following skills are necessary for independence in playing, owning, and receiving instruction on this instrument. The music teacher should confirm the need for those items, such as need for transport, which may not be necessary in all situations. The teacher should also add any items, such as the need to transport instructional materials to and from lessons, which may be applicable.

The therapist should indicate those requirements which a student is able to fulfill. The teacher or parents must provide for assistance in those areas in which a student may be dependent.

	Needed	Can Perform	Can Not Perform
1. Tune instrument			
2. Transport instrument			
3. Place instrument in case			
4. Open and close case			
5. Assemble instrument			
6. Disassemble instrument			
7. Clean instrument			
8. Apply lubricants			
9. Place instrument in playing position			
10. Align pieces			

FLUTE (C & E-flat)

C and E-flat flutes are considered together, as the same basic components are utilized. Differences are indicated in individual sections.

Considerations:
- General Body Position
- Major Body Parts Involved in Playing - Mobile/Stable Components - Functions of Major/Minor Joints Involved - Mobile/Stable Capacity

The flute is played in a manner requiring support *(stability)* and movement *(mobility)* of head/neck, trunk, and both upper extremities. The major individual joints required to function in a stable capacity are those of the neck, shoulders, elbows, and wrists. Movement is of major importance in the hands bilaterally, with the exception of the right thumb.

Considerations:
- Major Muscle Groups
- Movement Observed

Playing the flute utilizes muscle groups to produce stabilization of the neck, shoulders, and elbows held in a flexed, abducted, and internally rotated fashion. Wrists are stabilized in a slight extension and pronation with primary movements of fingers in flexion, extension, abduction, and adduction. Oral musculature produces lip closure and oral positioning for expelling wind. The degree of movement is greatest at the MP and IP joints bilaterally. Slight differences are noted in range of movement for the E-flat flute with decreases in shoulder abduction, wrist extension, and finger abduction bilaterally. Slight increase is noted in elbow flexion.

Considerations:
- Muscle Strength
- Speed/Dexterity

Muscle strength utilized bilaterally in playing the flute requires holding the instrument up against gravity; (Fair+ muscle grade) for periods of time. Additional strength is required for repetitive fingering (Good- to Good muscle grade), increasing with playing time. The speed/dexterity of fingers bilaterally relies on alternating, upward/downward movements, with isolated and coupled digit execution.

Considerations:
- Sensation
- Perception

Playing of the flute appears to utilize the deep sensations for positioning of arms and finger placement. Perceptual components appear to be in the areas of orientation and motor. Orientation mechanisms direct body movements in a planned and coordinated manner.

Considerations:
- Respiration
- Cardiac Output

The playing of the flute requires moderate exertion (light work), which may increase with prolonged playing.

Considerations:
- Vision
- Audition

The flute may be played by sighted individuals and also by those at any level of visual impairment. (Tactile/kinesthetic modalities may be primarily relied upon.) Auditory levels most functional are in the normal to moderate impairment range.

FLUTE (C & E-flat)

MAJOR MUSCLE GROUPS USED IN PLAYING
WITHOUT SUBSTITUTION OR ADAPTATION

KEY: B=Beginning Level   P=Held Position for Playing
        I =Intermediate Level   X=Muscle Movement Used in Playing
        A=Advanced Level   •=Increased Usage

Body Part	Function	Muscle or Muscle Groups	Left B	Left I	Left A	Right B	Right I	Right A
Face Mouth		Mentalis	x	—	—	x	—	—
Neck	Flexion & Rotation	Sternocleidomastoideus	x	—	—	x	—	—
Scapula	Elevation	Trapezius (Inferior)	p	—	—	p	—	—
Shoulder	Flexion	Deltoideus (Anterior)	p	—	—	p	—	—
	Abduction	Deltoideus (Middle)	p	—	—	p	—	—
	Internal Rotation	Internal Rotator Group	p	—	—	p	—	—
Elbow	Flexion	Biceps Brachii Brachialis	p	—	—	p	—	—
Forearm	Supination	Supinator Group	p	—	—	p	—	—
	Pronation	Pronator Group	—	—	—	p	—	—
Wrist	Deviation, Ulnar	Flexor Carpi Ulnaris Extensor Carpi Ulnaris Extensor Carpi Rad. Longus & Brevis	p	—	—	—	—	—
	Extension	Extensor Carpi Ulnaris	p	—	—	p	—	—

Body Part	Function	Muscle or Muscle Groups	Left B	Left I	Left A	Right B	Right I	Right A
Fingers	MP Flexion	Lumbricales	x	—	—	x	•	•
	IP Flexion (1st)	Flex. Digit. Superior	x	—	—	x	•	•
	IP Flexion (2nd)	Flex. Digit. Prof.	x	—	—	x	—	—
	MP Extension	Ext. Digit. Com.	x	—	—	x	—	—
	Adduction	Interossei Palmares	—	—	—	x	—	—
	Abduction	Interossei Dorsales	—	—	—	x	—	—
		Abduct. Digit. Min.	x	—	—	x	—	—
Thumb	MP Flexion	Flex. Poll. Brevis	x	—	—	x	—	—
	MP Extension	Ext. Poll. Brevis	—	—	—	x	—	—
	IP Extension	Ext. Poll. Longus	p	—	—	p	—	—
	Abduction	Abd. Poll. Brevis	x	—	—	—	—	—
		Abd. Poll. Longus	—	—	—	p	—	—
	Opposition		—	—	—		—	—

Muscles listed are used in the playing of this instrument; those not listed are not directly involved.

Facial and neck musculature is marked on right and left for convenience.
Increases (•) are noted in Intermediate Level and Advanced Level that are most obvious.
Muscles are used in groups for synergist movements rather than as isolated muscle movements.
Generally, X's in Beginning Level continue in Intermediate and Advanced Levels.

FLUTE (C & E-flat)

MOVEMENT OBSERVED IN PLAYING
(ACTIVE & POSITIONAL)
WITHOUT SUBSTITUTION OR ADAPTATION*

These ranges were determined through working with musicians. They reflect the musician's body size, individuality, and possibly style. The ranges are approximate to give a working baseline for instrument suitability.

Head/Neck:		Rotated (10°) and flexed (10°).
Shoulders:	Left	Flexed (50°) with internal rotation (60°).
	Right	Flexed (30°) with abduction (30°) and internal rotation (40°).
E-flat:	Right	Same as above except abduction (20°).
Elbows:	Left	Flexed (90°) with shoulder abduction and rotation.
	Right	Flexed (100°) with shoulder abduction and rotation.
E-flat:	Left	Flexed (110°) with shoulder abduction and rotation.
	Right	Flexed (110°) with shoulder abduction and rotation.
Forearms:	Left	Pronated (40°).
	Right	Pronated full range.
Wrists:	Left	Extended (60°) with Ulnar deviation (20°).
	Right	Extended (30°).
E-flat:	Left	Extended (45°).
	Right	Extended approximately the same as above.
Thumbs:	Left	Abducts (40-60°), held under index finger.
	Right	Abducted under index finger in functional resting fashion with flute held horizontal to palm.
Fingers:	Left	Flex MP (10–30°)
		Flex PIP (40-90°) index
		Flex PIP (40-60°) 3, 4, 5, fingers
		Flex DIP (30-90°) index
		Flex DIP (0-50°) 3, 4, 5, fingers with abduction.
	Right	Flex MP (10–30°), PIP (40-60°), DIP (20-60°), with slight abduction used during play.
E-flat:		Same as above, except decrease in abduction required during play.

*I.e., using normal body position for playing, without any devices for instrument or body parts.

Alto Saxophone in normal playing position

Hand position in play of Saxophone

Hand position in play of Saxophone

FAMILY: Woodwind
INSTRUMENT: Saxophone
TYPE: Alto and Tenor
MAKE: Buffet   Selmer
MODEL: Alto-Alto   Mark VII-Tenor
MATERIALS USED IN CONSTRUCTION: Metal

I.   Assembly and Disassembly
  A. Mechanical attachment
    1. Neck is friction-fitted to body with metal-to-metal contact and one clamping thumbscrew.
    2. Mouthpiece is friction-fitted to neck with plastic-to-lubricated-cork contact.
  B. Method of disassembly
    1. Adjacent pieces are grasped and pulled apart with a twisting motion against some resistance. Care must be taken to avoid damaging key mechanisms. The neck is held by friction fit and one small 8 mm x 15 mm (31 x 59 inches) thumbscrew which provides a clamping action. Thumbscrew must be loosened for disassembly.
    2. Reed is removed by loosening of ligature. See *Student Maintenance.*
  C. Method of assembly
    1. Adjacent pieces are grasped and pushed together with a twisting against some resistance. Care must be taken to avoid damaging key mechanisms. Thumbscrew at neck must be tightened.
    2. See *Student Maintenance* for reed assembly.
  D. Alignment of pieces
    Instruments are aligned through visual sighting of various keys and pieces in relation to one another. Adjacent pieces are grasped and twisted against some resistance. Care must be taken to avoid damaging key mechanisms. Two hands are needed to perform this operation.
  E. Neck Straps
    The weight of these instruments is supported with the assistance of a neck strap. This strap is placed over the head and hooked through a ring located on the instrument body. Length of strap is adjustable.

II. Tuning Requirements
    The saxophones are tuned by grasping the mouthpiece and neck and pulling them apart, or pushing them together, with a twisting motion against some resistance. Alignment of pieces must be maintained and care must be taken to avoid damaging key mechanisms.

III. Transport
    Both instruments are applied with a hard shell (wood composition) case which serves as a protective container during transport. Disassembly is required.

IV. Student Maintenance
  A. Tuning
    The instrument must be tuned both before and during play.
  B. Cleaning
    1. The instrument should be cleaned (wipe interior) after playing.
    2. Devices used: swab, swab on string
    Swab: The swab is essentially a stick with absorbent material placed at one end. It is passed through disassembled pieces.
    Swab on string: A weighted string which is attached to a cloth is dropped through one end of the disassembled instrument. The cloth is then drawn through.

Checklist

The following skills are necessary for independence in playing, owning, and receiving instruction on this instrument. The music teacher should confirm the need for those items, such as need for transport, which may not be necessary in all situations. The teacher should also add any items, such as the need to transport instructional materials to and from lessons, which may be applicable.

The therapist should indicate those requirements which a student is able to fulfill. The teacher or parents must provide for assistance in those areas in which a student may be dependent.

	Needed	Can Perform	Can Not Perform
1. Tune instrument	_____	_____	_____
2. Transport instrument	_____	_____	_____
3. Place instrument in case	_____	_____	_____
4. Open and close case	_____	_____	_____
5. Assemble instrument	_____	_____	_____
6. Disassemble instrument	_____	_____	_____
7. Clean instrument	_____	_____	_____
8. Apply lubricants	_____	_____	_____
9. Place instrument in playing position	_____	_____	_____
10. Align reeds	_____	_____	_____
11. Replace reeds	_____	_____	_____
12. Attach and adjust neck strap	_____	_____	_____

C. Lubrication

Joints must be periodically lubricated with a light-grade oil. Cork joint at mouthpiece must be lubricated with special grease.

D. Reed replacement

The reed is a piece of material, usually cane, which is the sound-producing agent of the instrument. It is fragile and usually protected by a metal sheath, which is placed over the mouthpiece when the instrument is idle. Reeds must be routinely replaced, often during play, and this requires the loosening of two small thumbscrews (8 mm x 10 mm) (.31 x .39 inches) which secure the ligature and reed to the mouthpiece. Replacement requires fine alignment of the new reed in relation to the mouthpiece with simultaneous tightening of the ligature.

The saxophone is a sophisticated mechanical device which requires the adjustment of rods, levers, and springs from time to time as well as replacement of parts such as key pads (found on the underside of keys and used to seal the opening between key and body of instrument) which are subject to deterioration. This work is referred to a highly skilled repair person and should be performed on a routine basis.

V. Variations Among Manufacturers

A. Dimensional variations are not considered significant.
B. Vinyl bags are available which will considerably diminish transport weight of alto saxophone. Bag is opened by a heavy zipper. Instrument protection is diminished.
C. Reeds and mouthpiece are available in various sizes and grades. Outside dimensions, however, are similar. Players report variation in breath pressures needed to play when using various combinations. Selection of an appropriate mouthpiece is musical as well as physical consideration.

SAXOPHONE (Alto/Tenor)

Alto and tenor saxophones are considered together, as the same basic components are utilized. Differences are indicated in individual sections.

Considerations:
- General Body Position
- Major Body Parts Involved in Playing - Mobile/Stable Components - Functions of Major/Minor Joints Involved - Mobile/ Stable Capacity

The saxophone is played in a manner requiring support *(stability)* and movement *(mobility)* of head/neck, trunk, and upper extremities. The major individual joints required to function in a stable capacity are those of the neck, shoulders, and elbows. Movement is of major importance in the joints of the hands except for the right thumb.

Considerations:
- Major Muscle Groups
- Movement Observed

The saxophone utilizes muscle groups to produce stabilization of the neck, scapulae, shoulders, and elbows held in a flexed, abducted, internally rotated fashion. Wrists are held in slight extension and pronated with primary movements of fingers in flexion, extension, abduction, and adduction. Oral musculature produces lip closure and oral positioning for expelling wind. The degree of movement is greatest in the MP joints bilaterally. Slight differences in range of movement are noted for alto saxophone, with increased elbow flexion and decreased finger abduction.

Considerations:
- Muscle Strength
- Speed/Dexterity

Muscle strength utilized bilaterally in playing the saxophone requires arms to be held up against gravity (Fair+ muscle grade) for periods of time. The weight of the instrument is held by a neck strap, requiring neck stability and strength adequate to support it. Additional strength is required for repetitive upward/downward fingering (Good- to Good muscle grade), increasing with playing time. The speed/ dexterity of fingers bilaterally relies upon alternating up/down and rolling movements with isolated, coupled, or mass digit execution.

Considerations:
- Sensation
- Perception

Playing the saxophone appears to utilize the deep sensations for positioning of arms and finger placement. Perceptual components appear to be in the areas of orientation and motor. Orientation mechanisms direct body movements in a planned and coordinated manner.

Considerations:
- Respiration
- Cardiac Output

The playing of the saxophone requires moderate exertion (light work), which may increase with prolonged playing.

Considerations:
- Vision
- Audition

The saxophone may be played by sighted individuals and also by those at any level of visual impairment. (Tactile/kinesthetic modalities may be primarily relied upon.) Auditory levels most functional are in the normal to moderate impairment range.

125

SAXOPHONE (Tenor/Alto)

MAJOR MUSCLE GROUPS USED IN PLAYING
WITHOUT SUBSTITUTION OR ADAPTATION

KEY: B=Beginning Level
I =Intermediate Level
A=Advanced Level

P=Held Position for Playing
X=Muscle Movement Used in Playing
•=Increased Usage

Body Part	Function	Muscle or Muscle Groups	Left B	Left I	Left A	Right B	Right I	Right A
Face Mouth		Mentalis						
		Orbicularis Oris	x			x		—
Neck	Flexion & Rotation	Sternocleidomastoideus	x			x		—
Scapula	Elevation	Trapezius (Inferior)	x			x		—
Shoulder	Flexion	Deltoideus (Anterior)	p			p		—
	Abduction	Deltoideus (Middle)	p			p		—
	Internal Rotation	Internal Rotator Group	p			p		—
Elbow	Flexion	Biceps Brachii						
		Brachialis	p	x	•	p		—
Forearm	Supination	Supinator Group	x	•	•	x		—
	Pronation	Pronator Group	x	•	•	x		—
Wrist	Extension	Extensor Carpi Ulnaris	x			x		—
	Flexion	Flexor Carpi Radial.						
		Flexor Carpi Ulnaris	x			x		—

Body Part	Function	Muscle or Muscle Groups	Left B	Left I	Left A	Right B	Right I	Right A
Fingers	MP Flexion	Lumbricales	x	—	—	x	—	—
	IP Flexion (1st)	Flex. Digit. Superior	x	—	—	x	—	—
	IP Flexion (2nd)	Flex. Digit. Prof.	x	—	—	x	—	—
	MP Extension	Ext. Digit. Com.	x	—	—	x	—	—
	Adduction	Interossei Palmares	x	—	—	x	—	—
	Abduction	Interossei Dorsales	—	—	—	x	—	—
	Abduction	Abduct. Digit. Min.	—	—	—	x	—	—
Thumb	MP Flexion	Flex. Poll. Brevis	x	—	—	—	—	—
	IP Flexion	Flex. Poll. Longus	x	—	—	—	—	—
	MP Extension	Ext. Poll. Brevis	x	—	—	—	—	—
	IP Extension	Ext. Poll Longus	x	—	—	—	—	—
	Abduction	Abd. Poll. Brevis	—	—	—	—	—	—
	Abduction	Abd. Poll. Longus	p	—	—	p	—	—
Trunk	Rotation	Obl. Ext. Abdominis	—	—	—	—	—	—
		Obl. Int. Abdominis	—	—	—	p	—	—

Muscles listed are used in the playing of this instrument; those not listed are not directly involved.

Facial and neck musculature is marked on right and left for convenience.
Increases (•) are noted in Intermediate Level and Advanced Level that are most obvious.
Muscles are used in groups for synergist movements rather than as isolated muscle movements.
Generally, X's in Beginning Level continue in Intermediate and Advanced Levels.

SAXOPHONE (Alto & Tenor)

MOVEMENT OBSERVED IN PLAYING
(ACTIVE & POSITIONAL)
WITHOUT SUBSTITUTION OR ADAPTATION*

These ranges were determined through working with musicians. They reflect the musician's body size, individuality, and possibly style. The ranges are approximate to give a working baseline for instrument suitability.

Instrument held to right side of body.

Head:		Flexed forward (20°).
Shoulders:	Left	Flexed (30°) with internal rotation (60°) at midline.
	Right	Flexed (10°) with abduction (20°), with internal rotation (20°).
Elbows: (Tenor)	Left	Flexed (60°) with shoulder flexion, abduction, and rotation.
	Right	Flexed (90°) with shoulder flexion, abduction, and rotation.
Elbows: (Alto)	Left	Flexed (90°) with shoulder flexion, abduction, and rotation.
	Right	Flexed (100°) with shoulder flexion, abduction, and rotation.
Forearms:	Left	Pronates (0–20°).
	Right	Pronates (20–40°).
Wrists:	Left	Extends (20–30°).
	Right	Extends (20–30°).
Thumbs:	Left	Abducted (60°) and flexes (0–20°).
	Right	Abducted (60°).
Fingers:	Left	Flexes MP (0–45°), PIP (20–60°), DIP (20–60°), with adjustments of abduction and adduction during play.
	Right	Flexes MP (0–40°), PIP (20–40°), DIP (0–40°), with adjustments of abduction and adduction during play. (Alto saxophone requires decrease in adjustments of finger abduction and adduction.)
Trunk		Slight rotation (20°) is required if instrument held at side of body.

*I.e., using normal body position for playing, without any devices for instrument or body parts.

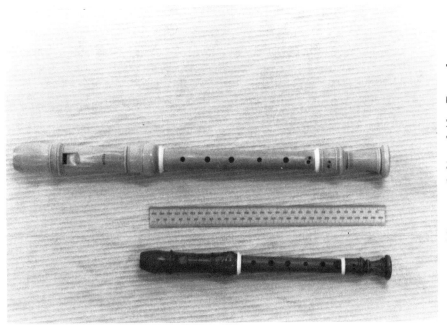

Comparison of Soprano (left) and Alto Recorders

Recorder in normal playing position

Hand position in play of Soprano Recorder

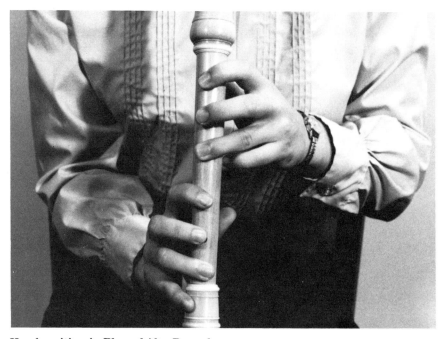

Hand position in Play of Alto Recorder

FAMILY: Woodwind
INSTRUMENT: Recorder
TYPE: Soprano   Alto
MAKE: Zen-On   Zen-On
MATERIALS USED IN CONSTRUCTION: Plastic

I.   Assembly and Disassembly
  A. Mechanical attachment
      Joints are friction-fitted with plastic-to-plastic surfaces.
  B. Method of disassembly
      Adjacent pieces are grasped and pulled apart with a twisting motion against some
      resistance.
  C. Method of assembly
      Adjacent pieces are grasped and pushed together with a twisting motion against
      some resistance.
  D. Alignment of pieces
      Instruments are aligned through visual sighting of various pieces in relation to one
      another. Adjacent pieces are grasped and twisted against some resistance. Two
      hands are needed for this operation. Bottom joint may be adjusted several degress in
      order to accommodate individual differences in the fifth finger of the right hand.

II. Tuning Requirements
      The recorder is tuned by grasping the mouthpiece and barrel and pulling them apart,
      or pushing them together, with a twisting motion against some resistance. Align-
      ment of pieces must be maintained.

III. Transport
      The instrument is supplied with a hard shell (plastic) case, which serves as a protec-
      tive container during transport. Disassembly is required.

IV. Student Maintenance
  A. Tuning
      The instrument must be tuned both before and during play.
  B. Cleaning
      1. The instrument should be cleaned (wipe interior) after playing.
      2. Device used: swab. The swab is a stick with absorbent material attached to one
          end. It is passed through each length of the disassembled instrument.
      Note: The instrument may become clogged during play by the passage of saliva or
      internal condensation. Instrument must be cleared by cleaning or blowing while
      finger is placed over window. Some manufacturers recommend drawing air through
      the instrument. Application of a surfactant (surface lubricant) such as Dupenol to the
      bore may relieve this problem on wooden instruments.

V.   Variation Among Manufacturers
  A. Materials
      Recorders are manufactured in both wood and plastic. Plastic instruments are gen-
      erally lighter and easier to maintain.
  B. Number of pieces
      Two-piece recorders are common. No adjustment of the holes for the fifth finger of the
      right hand is possible on these instruments.
  C. Dimensions
      Length, diameter, and hole spacings vary from maker to maker. These differences
      may not be significant for the soprano, but an alto should be examined for the
      amount of "stretch" required to cover the holes. The alto examined is comfortable for
      most adult players.

D. Cases
Cloth pouches, closed with a button, are available for the soprano recorder. Disassembly is not required if this type of cover is used but instrument protection is diminished.
E. Thumb rest
Some recorders are marketed with an integral support device which rests upon the thumb of the right hand. Such devices may be purchased for nominal cost and are easily attached.

Instrument: Recorder (Soprano or Alto)

Checklist

The following skills are necessary for independence in playing, owning, and receiving instruction on this instrument. The music teacher should confirm the need for those items, such as need for transport, which may not be necessary in all situations. The teacher should also add any items, such as the need to transport instructional materials to and from lessons, which may be applicable.

The therapist should indicate those requirements which a student is able to fulfill. The teacher or parents must provide for assistance in those areas in which a student may be dependent.

	Needed	Can Perform	Can Not Perform
1. Tune instrument	_____	_____	_____
2. Transport instrument	_____	_____	_____
3. Place instrument in case	_____	_____	_____
4. Open and close case	_____	_____	_____
5. Assemble instrument	_____	_____	_____
6. Disassemble instrument	_____	_____	_____
7. Clean instrument	_____	_____	_____
8. Apply lubricants	_____	_____	_____
9. Place instrument in playing position	_____	_____	_____
10. Align pieces	_____	_____	_____

RECORDER (Soprano/Alto)

Both alto and soprano recorders are included, as the same basic movements are used in playing. Differences are indicated in individual sections.

Considerations:
- General Body Position
- Major Body Parts Involved in Playing - Mobile/Stable Components - Functions of Major/Minor Joints Involved - Mobile/ Stable Capacity

The recorder is played in a manner requiring support *(stability)* and movement *(mobility)* of head/neck, trunk, and upper extremities. The major individual joints required to function in a stable capacity are those of the neck and right thumb, supported by shoulders, elbows, and wrists. Movement is of major importance in the joints of the fingers of the right hand and the first three fingers of the left hand.

Considerations:
- Major Muscle Groups
- Movement Observed

The recorder utilizes muscle groups to produce stability of shoulders and elbows held in a flexed and internally rotated holding position. Movement is produced in the fingers of both hands and the thumb of the left hand. The degree of movement is greatest in the fingers at the MP and IP joints. Slight differences in degree of movement are noted for the soprano recorder. There is an increase of elbow flexion and wrist extension, and a decrease in finger abduction, thumb abduction, and left wrist deviation. Oral musculature produces lip closure and oral position for expelling wind.

Considerations:
- Muscle Strength
- Speed/Dexterity

Muscle strength utilized bilaterally in playing requires holding the instrument (thumb support included) up against gravity (Fair+ muscle grade) for periods of time. Additional strength is required for the repeated lifting of fingers up and down to cover openings (Good- muscle grade), increasing with prolonged playing. The speed and dexterity of fingers requires alternating up and down, and rolling movements with isolated and coupled digit execution.

Considerations:
- Sensation
- Perception

Playing the recorder appears to utilize the deep sensations for finger movements and tactile discrimination for finger placement. Perceptual components appear to be in the areas of orientation and motor. Orientation mechanisms direct body movements in a planned, coordinated manner.

Considerations:
- Respiration
- Cardiac Output

The playing of the recorder requires moderate exertion (light work), which may increase with prolonged playing.

Considerations:
- Vision
- Audition

The recorder may be played by sighted individuals and also by those at any level of visual impairment. (Tactile/kinesthetic modalities may be primarily relied upon.) Auditory levels most functional are in the normal to moderate impairment range.

RECORDER (Soprano/Alto)

MAJOR MUSCLE GROUPS USED IN PLAYING
WITHOUT SUBSTITUTION OR ADAPTATION

KEY:
B=Beginning Level
I=Intermediate Level
A=Advanced Level

P=Held Position for Playing
X=Muscle Movement Used in Playing
•=Increased Usage

Body Part	Function	Muscle or Muscle Groups	Left B	Left I	Left A	Right B	Right I	Right A
Face Mouth		Mentalis	x	—	—	x	—	—
Scapula	Elevation	Trapezius (Inferior)	p	—	—	p	—	—
Shoulder	External Rotation	External Rotator Group		—	—	p	—	—
	Internal Rotation	Internal Rotator Group	p	—	—	p	—	—
Elbow	Flexion	Biceps Brachii Brachialis	p	—	—	p	—	—
Forearm	Pronation	Pronator Group	p	—	—	p	—	—
Wrist	Deviation, Radial	Flexor Carpi Radial. Extensor Carpi Rad. Longus Extensor Carpi Rad. Brevis	p	—	—		—	—
	Extension	Extensor Carpi Ulnaris	p	—	—	p	—	—
	Flexion	Flexor Carpi Radial. Flexor Carpi Ulnaris	p	—	—	p	—	—

Body Part	Function	Muscle or Muscle Groups	Left B	Left I	Left A	Right B	Right I	Right A
Fingers	MP Flexion	Lumbricales	x	—	—	x	—	—
	IP Flexion (1st)	Flex. Digit. Superior	x	—	—	x	—	—
	IP Flexion (2nd)	Flex. Digit. Prof.	x	—	—	x	—	—
	MP Extension	Ext. Digit. Com.	x	—	—	x	—	—
	Abduction	Interossei Dorsales	x	—	—		—	—
Thumb	MP Flexion	Flex. Poll. Brevis	x	—	—		—	—
	IP Flexion	Flex. Poll. Longus	x	—	—		—	—
	MP Extension	Ext. Poll. Brevis	x	—	—		—	—
	IP Extension	Ext. Poll. Longus	x	—	—		—	—
	Abduction	Abd. Poll. Brevis		—	—		—	—
		Abd. Poll. Longus	x	—	—	p	—	—

Muscles listed are used in the playing of this instrument; those not listed are not directly involved.

Facial and neck musculature is marked on right and left for convenience.
Increases (•) are noted in Intermediate Level and Advanced Level that are most obvious.
Muscles are used in groups for synergist movements rather than as isolated muscle movements.
Generally, X's in Beginning Level continue in Intermediate and Advanced Levels.

RECORDER (Soprano)

MOVEMENT OBSERVED IN PLAYING
(ACTIVE & POSITIONAL)
WITHOUT SUBSTITUTION OR ADAPTATION*

These ranges were determined through working with musicians. They reflect the musician's body size, individuality, and possibly style. The ranges are approximate to give a working baseline for instrument suitability.

Head:		Neutral.
Shoulders:		Held in neutral (at sides) with internal rotation (60°).
Elbows:	Left	Flexed (120°) with rotation.
	Right	Flexed (100°) with rotation.
Forearms:		Pronated (30°).
Wrists:		Extended (45°).
Thumbs:	Left	MP flexes (0-20°) with abduction (20°), IP (0-20°).
	Right	Abducted (20°).
Fingers:		Flex MP (0-30°), PIP (0-45°), DIP (0-20°). (Except 5th on left not used to play.)

*I.e., using normal body position for playing, without any devices for instrument or body parts.

RECORDER (Alto)

MOVEMENT OBSERVED IN PLAYING
(ACTIVE & POSITIONAL)
WITHOUT SUBSTITUTION OR ADAPTATION*

These ranges were determined through working with musicians. They reflect the musician's body size, individuality, and possibly style. The ranges are approximate to give a working baseline for instrument suitability.

Head:		Neutral position.
Shoulders:	Left	Held in neutral (at sides) with internal rotation (60°) to midline.
Elbows:	Left	Flexed (100°) with internal rotation.
	Right	Flexed (90°) with internal rotation.
Forearms:		Pronated (30°).
Wrists:		Extended (30°) with slight radial deviation on left.
Thumbs:	Left	MP flexes (0–30°) with abduction (40°), IP (0–30°).
	Right	Abducted (40°).
Fingers:		Flex MP (0–30°), PIP (0–45°), DIP (0–20°) with slight abduction and adduction used, especially on right 5th finger. (Fifth finger on left not used to play.)

Note: Hands may be reversed.

*I.e., using normal body position for playing, without any devices for instrument or body parts.

FAMILY:	PERCUSSION
INSTRUMENTS:	CRASH CYMBALS
	TIMBALI
	TRAP SET
	TIMPANI
	XYLOPHONE
	MARIMBA
	VIBRAPHONE

INTRODUCTION

Note: There are in excess of forty common percussion instruments in use today. The particular instruments detailed here were selected for their practicality, availability, and ease of use in class or ensemble settings.

The percussion instruments produce sound as a result of being struck. They have been categorized by many different criteria. The most common division has been into instruments which are capable of producing exact pitch and those which are not. However, many instruments may fall into either category, depending upon their specific musical usage. For purposes of analysis, the percussion instruments will be divided here into two categories: Ideophones and Membranophones.

Ideophone instruments produce sound through vibrations set up within the physical body of the instrument. These instruments require little, if any, physical manipulation on the part of the player other than those skills needed in the act of playing.

Some of these instruments produce sounds of exact pitch when a bar of metal, wood, or synthetic material has been struck by a mallet. Bars are tuned by adjusting their length, width, or thickness and are usually arranged in the same manner as a piano keyboard, e.g., bars nearest the player are evenly spaced while those more distant are grouped in alternate sets of twos and threes.

The marimba, xylophone, and vibraphone form part of this group. Each of these instruments has a resonating tube located beneath each bar. The resonating tubes are essentially pipes, open at one end, which amplify the bars' sound.

The vibraphone has disks located within each resonating tube. These disks are spun by a small electric motor. The spinning disks cause the tone of each note to waver slightly. This controlled variation of tone is called vibrato. Since the bars of the vibraphone are made of metal, they tend to sound for long periods of time. The instrument is equipped with a pedal-operated damper, which the player can use to control resonating time.

Instruments of inexact pitch produce sound when struck by hand, stick, mallet, or other instrument component. There are hundreds of percussion instruments which fit into this category, all of which fulfill a musical, even if somewhat limited, function.

The cymbals are part of this group. The sounding agents are the cymbals themselves. Vibrations are set up by striking the cymbals together, or with a stick.

Membranophone instruments produce sound through vibrations set up on a tensioned membrane. These instruments may require considerable manipulation of instrument components by the player in addition to those skills needed in the act of playing.

The tone produced may be of exact or inexact pitch. A given instrument's capacity to produce exact pitch is determined by the structure of the shell over which the membrane is tensioned. The membrane may be of natural (usually calfskin) or synthetic (usually Mylar) material.

The various drums that are part of the trap set are members of this group and are not generally tuned to any exact pitch. The timbali may or may not be tuned to pitch. The timpani are designed to be tuned to exact pitch within a considerable range and to be retuned rapidly during play.

INSTRUMENT SELECTION GUIDE

An "X" indicates a potential physical limitation in relationship to "normal" use of the instrument. The presence of an "X" should not necessarily preclude consideration of the instrument if compensatory techniques and adaptations are appropriate.

Potential Limitations	Crash Cymbals	Timbali	Trap Set	Timpani	Xylophone	Marimba	Vibraphone
Contractures of							
Neck							
Shoulders	X	X	X	X	X	X	X
Elbows	X	X	X	X	X	X	X
Wrists	X	X	X	X	X	X	X
Fingers	X	X	X	X	X	X	X
Hips	X			X	X	X	X
Knees	X			X	X	X	X
Ankles	X		X	X	X	X	X
Incoordination							
Gross - Upper Extremities	X	X	X	X	X	X	X
- Lower Extremities			X		X	X	X
Fine - Upper Extremities	X	X	X	X	X	X	X
- Lower Extremities			X				
Limb Loss (prosthesis fit implied)							
- Upper Extremities							
- Above Elbow	X	X	X	X	X	X	X
- Below Elbow	X	X	X	X	X	X	X
- Partial Hand	X	X	X	X	X	X	X

Potential Limitations	Crash Cymbals	Timbali	Trap Set	Timpani	Xylophone	Marimba	Vibraphone
- Lower Extremities							
- Above Knee	X		X	X	X	X	X
- Below Knee	X		X	X	X	X	X
- Symes	X		X	X	X	X	X
- Partial Foot	X		X	X	X	X	X
- Hip Disarticulation	X		X	X	X	X	X
Movement							
Athetoid - Upper Extremities	X	X	X	X	X	X	X
- Lower Extremities	X		X		X	X	X
Rigidity - Upper Extremities	X	X	X	X	X	X	X
- Lower Extremities	X		X		X	X	X
Fluctuating Tone							
- Upper Extremities	X	X	X	X	X	X	X
- Lower Extremities	X		X		X	X	X
Tremor							
Resting - Upper Extremities	X	X	X		X	X	X
Intention - Upper Extremities	X	X	X	X	X	X	X
Dysmetria - Upper Extremities	X	X	X	X	X	X	X
Pain	X	X	X	X	X	X	X
Perception - Children							
Apraxia	X	X	X	X	X	X	X
Posture & Bilateral Integration	X	X	X	X	X	X	X
Space Visual	X	X	X	X	X	X	X
- Adults							
Neglect	X	X	X	X	X	X	X
Hemianopsia	X	X	X	X	X	X	X
Spatial	X	X	X	X	X	X	X
Apraxia	X	X	X	X	X	X	X

Potential Limitations	Crash Cymbals	Timbali	Trap Set	Timpani	Xylophone	Marimba	Vibraphone
Sensation							
Tactile	X	X	X	X	X	X	X
Proprioception	X	X	X	X	X	X	X
Kinesthesia	X	X	X	X	X	X	X
Spasticity - Upper Extremities	X	X	X	X	X	X	X
- Lower Extremities			X	X	X	X	X
Weakness							
Proximal - Head/Neck				X			
- Shoulder	X	X	X	X	X	X	X
- Trunk	X	X	X	X	X	X	X
Distal - Upper Extremities	X	X	X	X	X	X	X
- Lower Extremities	X		X	X	X	X	X

FAMILY: Percussion
INSTRUMENT: Crash Cymbals
SIZE: 18 Inches
TYPE: Band or Orchestra
MAKE: Zildjian
MATERIALS USED IN CONSTRUCTION: Metal

I.   Assembly and Disassembly
      None

II.   Tuning Requirements
      None

III. Transport
      The cymbals are not provided with a case when purchased.

IV.   Student Maintenance
      Occasional wiping

V.   Variation Among Manufacturers
      A. Sizes
          304.8 mm to 609.6 mm (12 to 24 inches)
      B. Handles
          Handles may vary in design. Most common is a flaccid loop of leather or plastic. A
          T-shaped handle of wood and metal is also available.

Checklist

The following skills are necessary for independence in playing, owning, and receiving instruction on this instrument. The music teacher should confirm the need for those items, such as need for transport, which may not be necessary in all situations. The teacher should also add any items, such as the need to transport instructional materials to and from lessons, which may be applicable.

The therapist should indicate those requirements which a student is able to fulfill. The teacher or parents must provide for assistance in those areas in which a student may be dependent.

	Needed	Can Perform	Can Not Perform
1. Transport instrument	————	————————	————

CRASH CYMBALS

Considerations:
- General Body Position
- Major Body Parts Involved in Playing - Mobile/Stable Components - Functions of Major/Minor Joints Involved - Mobile/ Stable Capacity

The cymbals are played in a manner requiring support *(stability)* and movement *(mobility)* of trunk and upper extremities. The major individual joints required to function in a stable capacity are those of the hands. Movement is of major importance in the joints of the shoulders, elbow, and forearms.

Considerations:
- Major Muscle Groups
- Movement Observed

The cymbals utilize muscle groups to produce stabilization, flexion, abduction, rotation, and pronation of both upper extremities. The wrists are held in extension with fingers flexed around handles. Movement is greatest for shoulders bilaterally, and used to a lesser degree in elbows and forearms. *(Note:* Method of play was by striking cymbals in a vertical position, then turning them to a horizontal position with inner surfaces toward the floor.)

Considerations:
- Muscle Strength
- Speed/Dexterity

Muscle strength utilized bilaterally in playing the cymbals requires holding the instrument up against gravity (Fair+ to Good- muscle grade) while playing. Additional strength is required during striking and holding (palms down) for tone (Good- to Good). Dexterity requirements involves fine upper extremity adjustment when several crashes are performed.

Considerations:
- Sensation
- Perception

Playing the cymbals appears to utilize the deep sensations for arm movements. Perceptual components appear to be in the areas of orientation, visual, and motor. (Exclude vision for non-sighted individuals). Orientation mechanisms direct body movements, using visual cues in a planned, coordinated manner.

Considerations:
- Respiration
- Cardiac Output

The playing of the cymbals requires moderate exertion (light work), which may increase with prolonged playing. Respiration must be adequate to maintain level of exertion without fatigue.

Considerations:
- Vision
- Audition

The cymbals may be played by sighted individuals and also by those at any level of visual impairment. (Tactile/kinesthetic modalities may be primarily relied upon.) Auditory levels most functional are in the normal to moderate impairment range.

MAJOR MUSCLE GROUPS USED IN PLAYING
WITHOUT SUBSTITUTION OR ADAPTATION

KEY:
B=Beginning Level
I =Intermediate Level
A=Advanced Level

P=Held Position for Playing
X=Muscle Movement Used in Playing
• =Increased Usage

Body Part	Function	Muscle or Muscle Groups	Left B	Left I	Left A	Right B	Right I	Right A
Scapula	Elevation	Trapezius (Interior)	x			x		
Shoulder	Flexion	Deltoideus (Anterior)	x			x		
	Abduction	Deltoideus (Middle)	x			x		
	External Rotation	External Rotator Group	x			x		
	Internal Rotation	Internal Rotator Group	x			x		
Elbow	Flexion	Biceps Brachii	x			x		
		Brachialis	x			x		
Forearm	Supination	Supinator Group	x			x		
	Pronation	Pronator Group	X			X		
Wrist	Extension	Extensor Carpi Ulnaris	p			p		
	Flexion	Flexor Carpi Radial.						
		Flexor Carpi Ulnaris	p			p		
Fingers	MP Flexion	Lumbricales	p			p		
	IP Flexion (1st)	Flex. Digit. Superior	p			p		
	IP Flexion (2nd)	Flex. Digit. Prof.	p			p		
	Abduction	Interossei Palmares	p			p		
		Interossei Dorsales						
	Adduction	Abduct. Digit. Min.	p			p		

Muscles listed are used in the playing of this instrument; those not listed are not directly involved.

Facial and neck musculature is marked on right and left for convenience.
Increases (•) are noted in Intermediate Level and Advanced Level that are most obvious.
Muscles are used in groups for synergist movements rather than as isolated muscle movements.
Generally, X's in Beginning Level continue in Intermediate and Advanced Levels.

CRASH CYMBALS

MOVEMENT OBSERVED IN PLAYING
(ACTIVE & POSITIONAL)
WITHOUT SUBSTITUTION OR ADAPTATION*

These ranges were determined through working with musicians. They reflect the musician's body size, individuality, and possibly style. The ranges are approximate to give a working baseline for instrument suitability.

Head: Neutral position.

Shoulders: Flexes (0–40°), with abduction (0–60°) and internal rotation (0–40°), degree increasing after cymbals struck and held for tone.

Elbows: Flexes (90–70°), degree decreases after cymbals struck.

Forearms: Held in neutral (0°) at midline to strike full range of pronation following.

Wrists: Held in functional resting fashion (20°) of extension.

Thumbs: Adducted to handle.

Fingers: Full range of flexion into a fist for holding handles.

*I.e., using normal body position for playing, without any devices for instrument or body parts.

FAMILY: Percussion
INSTRUMENT: Timbali
MAKE: Ludwig
MODEL: No model specification
MATERIALS USED IN CONSTRUCTION: Metal shell, plastic playing heads

I. Assembly and Disassembly
The timbali are retained by a slot (on side of drum) and tongue (on stand) arrangement. The drums are lifted from the stand. There are no other mechanical attachments. The stand is collapsible and adjustable through the turning of two wing bolts which exert clamping pressure.

II. Tuning Requirements
The timbali are tuned to various pitches. Range of pitch is dependent upon size of instrument. Tuning is accomplished by turning the metal bolts (tension rods) which are located around the circumference of each drum. A special wrench, known as a tuning key, is supplied for this purpose. The tuning key is placed over the end of each tension rod and turned in a clockwise or counterclockwise direction against resistance.
Note: A drum which has a playing surface (head) that is made of plastic is stable, once tuned. Drums equipped with skin (calf or goat) playing heads respond to changes in temperature and humidity; frequent retuning is necessary.

III. Transport
Drums must be removed from stand for easy transport. Stand may be folded by loosening two wing nuts. Two hands are needed for this operation. Cases are not provided for the instrument.

IV. Student Maintenance
Playing surfaces (heads) deteriorate with age and need replacement. They may also split due to improper tuning, or overly energetic playing. Head replacement involves the loosening and removal of all tension rods, using the tuning key and removing the metal ring (rim or counterhoop) which is retained by the tension rods and encircles the circumference of the drum. The rim retains the head in position. Once the rim is removed, the head can be lifted off. A new head is set in place. The rim is then replaced and the tension rods run through their respective holes. The threaded ends of the rods are aligned with their retaining holes and tightened with the tuning key.
Note: Although this process is generally performed by the student, the need for head replacement is infrequent if proper care has been exercised in maintaining and playing the instrument.

V. Variation Among Manufacturers
Sizes, tuning mechanisms, and stands are similar to those of the instrument discussed here.

Checklist

The following skills are necessary for independence in playing, owning, and receiving instruction on this instrument. The music teacher should confirm the need for those items, such as need for transport, which may not be necessary in all situations. The teacher should also add any items, such as the need to transport instructional materials to and from lessons, which may be applicable.

The therapist should indicate those requirements which a student is able to fulfill. The teacher or parents must provide for assistance in those areas in which a student may be dependent.

	Needed	Can Perform	Can Not Perform
1. Tune instrument	_____	_____	_____
2. Transport instrument	_____	_____	_____
3. Adjust position of instrument	_____	_____	_____
4. Assemble instrument	_____	_____	_____
5. Disassemble instrument	_____	_____	_____
6. Remove and replace damaged heads	_____	_____	_____
7. Place sticks in hands	_____	_____	_____
8. Change sticks if necessary	_____	_____	_____
9. Retrieve dropped sticks	_____	_____	_____

TIMBALI

Considerations:
- General Body Position
- Major Body Parts Involved in Playing - Mobile/Stable Components - Functions of Major/Minor Joints Involved - Mobile/Stable Capacity

The timbali are played in a manner requiring support *(stability)* and movement *(mobility)* of trunk and both upper extremities. The major individual joints required to function in a stable capacity are those of the trunk and hands. Movement is of major importance in the joints of the shoulder, elbows, and wrists.

Considerations:
- Major Muscle Groups
- Movement Observed

The timbali utilize muscle groups to produce stability, flexion, abduction, rotation, pronation, and supination of the upper extremities. Wrist movement (one technique) includes a rotary synergy of flexion, extension, and deviation. Hands are held in a flexed position (right palm down, left thumb upward) around sticks. The degree of movement is greatest for shoulders, elbows and wrists.

Considerations:
- Muscle Strength
- Speed/Dexterity

Muscle strength utilized bilaterally in playing the timbali requires holding drum sticks up against gravity (Fair+ muscle grade), while moving in various directions for periods of time. Additional strength is required for drumming technique using repeated arm movements (Good- to Good muscle grade). The speed/dexterity utilized in arm and wrist movements is a very fine motor control requiring rapid, repetitive, alternating movements, increasing with advanced playing.

Considerations:
- Sensation
- Perception

Playing the timbali appears to utilize the deep sensations for arm movements. Perceptual components appear to be in the areas of orientation, visual, and motor. Orientation mechanisms direct body movements using visual cues in a planned, coordinated manner. (A significant degree of perceptual skills is employed and individuals lacking in visual skills may encounter difficulty.)

Considerations:
- Respiration
- Cardiac Output

The playing of the timbali requires moderate exertion (light work), which may increase with prolonged playing. Respiration must be adequate to maintain level of exertion without signs of fatigue.

Considerations:
- Vision
- Audition

The timbali appear to rely on vision skills, with most functional levels from normal to moderately low vision. Auditory levels most functional are in the normal to moderate impairment range.

TIMBALI

MAJOR MUSCLE GROUPS USED IN PLAYING
WITHOUT SUBSTITUTION OR ADAPTATION

KEY: B=Beginning Level   P=Held Position for Playing
          I =Intermediate Level   X=Muscle Movement Used in Playing
          A=Advanced Level   • =Increased Usage

Body Part	Function	Muscle or Muscle Groups	Left B	Left I	Left A	Right B	Right I	Right A
Scapula	Elevation	Trapezius (Inferior)	x	—	—	x	—	—
Shoulder	Flexion	Deltoideus (Anterior)	x	—	—	x	—	—
	Abduction	Deltoideus (Middle)	x	—	—	x	—	—
	External Rotation	External Rotator Group	x	•	•	x	•	•
	Internal Rotation	Internal Rotator Group	x	•	•	x	•	•
Elbow	Flexion	Biceps Brachii	x	—	—	x	—	—
		Brachialis						
Forearm	Supination	Supinator Group	x	•	•	x	•	•
	Pronation	Pronator Group	x	•	•	x	•	•
Wrist	Deviation, Radial	Flexor Carpi Radial.	x			x		
		Extensor Carpi Rad. Longus						
		Extensor Carpi Rad. Brevis						
	Deviation, Ulnar	Flexor Carpi Ulnaris	x			x		
		Extensor Carpi Ulnaris						
	Extension	Extensor Carpi Rad. Longus & Brevis	x			x		
		Extensor Carpi Ulnaris	x			x		
	Flexion	Flexor Carpi Radial.	x			x		
		Flexor Carpi Ulnaris	x			x		

			Left			Right		
Body Part	**Function**	**Muscle or Muscle Groups**	**B**	**I**	**A**	**B**	**I**	**A**
Fingers	MP Flexion	Lumbricales	p	—	—	p	—	—
	IP Flexion (1st)	Flex. Digit. Superior	p	—	—	p	—	—
	IP Flexion (2nd)	Flex. Digit. Prof.	p	—	—	p	—	—
	Adduction	Interossei Palmares	p	—	—	p	—	—
Thumb	MP Flexion	Flex. Poll. Brevis	p	—	—	p	—	—
	IP Flexion	Flex. Poll. Longus	p	—	—	p	—	—
	Abduction	Abd. Poll. Brevis						
		Abd. Poll. Longus	p	—	—	p	—	—

Muscles listed are used in the playing of this instrument; those not listed are not directly involved.

Facial and neck musculature is marked on right and left for convenience.
Increases (•) are noted in Intermediate Level and Advanced Level that are most obvious.
Muscles are used in groups for synergist movements rather than as isolated muscle movements.
Generally, X's in Beginning Level continue in Intermediate and Advanced Levels.

TIMBALI

MOVEMENT OBSERVED IN PLAYING
(ACTIVE & POSITIONAL)
WITHOUT SUBSTITUTION OR ADAPTATION*

These ranges were determined through working with musicians. They reflect the musician's body size, individuality, and possibly style. The ranges are approximate to give a working baseline for instrument suitability.

Head:		Held in neutral position.
Shoulders:		Flex (20–40°), with abduction (0–40°) and internal rotation (0–45°).
Elbows:		Flexes (70-100°) with abduction and rotation.
Forearms:	Left	Pronates (0–30°).
	Right	Pronates (0–40°) and supinates (0–40°).
Wrists:		Held in neutral with alternate use of ulnar deviation (0-20°) and radial deviation (0-10°) as sticks are bounced against palm surface.
Thumbs:		Abducted and held under index finger.
Fingers:	Left	Flexed around stick in fist fashion, MP (60°), PIP (90°), DIP (60°).
	Right	Flexed around stick in a pronated prehension (tripod) position, MP (60°), PIP (50°), DIP (20°).

*I.e., using normal body position for playing, without any devices for instrument or body parts.

Snare Drum in normal (seated) playing position (mallet grip)

Trap Set in normal playing position, sticks held in traditional grip

Snare Drum in normal (seated) playing position, traditional grip

Trap Set (left to right) Hi-Hat Cymbal (with pedal), Tom-Tom Drum mounted on Bass Drum (with pedal), Snare Drum on stand, ride Cymbal, Floor Tom-Tom Drum, stool in front

Left hand stick position

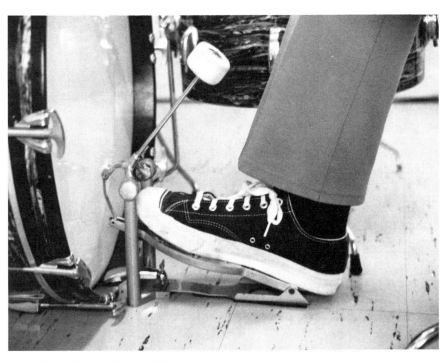

Bass Drum Foot pedal position

FAMILY: Percussion
INSTRUMENT: Trap Set
MAKE: Ludwig
MODEL: Classic
MATERIALS USED IN CONSTRUCTION: Wooden Shells, Plastic Playing Heads

The trap set is actually an assemblage of several different percussion instruments arranged in such a way that a single player can strike one or several of the available instruments. Special hardware has been designed for trap sets to enable the player to utilize hands and feet for the simultaneous playing of several instruments as well as to arrange the position of components to suit individual needs. Drums, hardware, and cymbals are generally considered separate items when purchasing a trap set; however, for purposes of analysis each sounding component (drums and cymbals) will be considered together with its support or playing component (hardware).

Drum measurements are standardized among manufacturers. A two-number system is used. A snare drum may be described as 5-1/2 x 14 inches. The first number denotes the distance between playing heads. The second number denotes the diameter of the playing head. Manufacturers are in the process of converting to the metric system but catalogs are generally still in inches. The figure 5-1/4 x 14 inches would become 139.7 x 355.6 mm; therefore, measurements will be expressed in inches, then converted to metric. One inch equals 25.4 mm. This measuring system does not indicate the amount of space actually occupied by a drum since the rim (metal ring which retains drum head) rises above the playing head and other parts extend the diameter. The outside dimensions of the 5-1/2 x 14 inch snare drum are actually 6 x 15-1/2 inches.

Parts are as follows:
    A. Bass drum with spurs, pedal and tom-tom holder
        The bass drum rests on the floor and is the largest single item of the trap set. The spurs are retractable metal rods, held by wing bolts, which prevent the drum from rolling. The bass drum pedal is clamped to the rim of the drum by a wing bolt. The right foot is generally used to depress the spring-loaded pedal, causing a beater to strike the drum head and return. Pedal travel is approximately 3.15 inches (80 mm). The tom-tom holder is mounted on the upper portion of the bass drum. It may be adjusted in four different directions through the use of a special wrench which is provided with the trap set. Adjustments are clamp type and require considerable torque in order to support weight of tom-tom.
    B. Tom-tom with mount
        The drum is attached to the bass drum mount. An additional mount component is attached to the side of the drum and allows two further adjustments. Adjustment involves additional use of wrench supplied.
    C. Floor tom-tom
        The drum is supported by three individually adjustable legs. Legs are tightened in position through the use of wing nuts. Playing surface (head) may also be set at a slight angle (25 degrees). Height is adjustable from 17.32 inches to 26.77 inches (440 mm to 680 mm).
    D. Snare drum and stand
        The snare drum is mounted on a folding stand which is adjustable for height and angle of playing surface. Erection of the stand involves tightening of one wing bolt to hold legs in position, one wing nut to maintain angle of playing surface, and one nut with handles which clamps the snare drum to the stand. Height of the playing surface may be adjusted from 26.18 inches (665 mm) to 34.65 inches (880 mm) above the floor. Angle of playing surface can be adjusted from 10 degrees to 45 degrees (0 degrees is considered parallel with floor).
        Note: This range is far beyond adjustments necessary or desirable for play.

E. Ride cymbal with stand

This cymbal is mounted on a telescoping stand which also allows for adjusting the angle of the cymbal. The stand is erected by tightening one wing bolt to secure legs, two wing bolts to secure the telescoping sections, one wing bolt to adjust angle of cymbal, and one wing nut to secure cymbal to stand. Stand is adjustable in height from 21.26 inches to 53.54 inches (540 mm to 1360 mm) above the floor. Angle of cymbal can be adjusted from 315 degrees to 45 degrees (0 degrees is considered parallel with floor.)

Note: This range is far beyond adjustment necessary or desirable for play.

F. One pair hi-hat cymbals and hi-hat stand

The stand separates these cymbals with playing surface nearly parallel. Depressing a spring-loaded pedal at the bottom of the stand causes a connecting rod to bring the higher cymbal in contact with its stationary partner. The left foot is generally used on this pedal. The hi-hat stand is erected by tightening one wing bolt to secure legs, guiding a steel shaft into a retaining hole to maintain pedal position, tightening a wing bolt, adjusting a retractable spur through the use of another wing bolt, screwing two pieces of the connecting rod together, clamping a steel shaft which contains the connecting rod with a wing bolt in position, and placing the stationary cymbal at the top of the shaft. The moving cymbal is held by a mechanism consisting of one wing bolt, one locking wing nut, two felt washers, and two threaded washers. Spring pressure is adjustable by turning a large threaded washer located above the pedal. Angle of lower cymbal can be adjusted by a long thumbscrew. Height and separation of both cymbals can be adjusted by movement of steel shaft and upper cymbal retaining piece (clutch).

G. Drum stool

The trap set is played while seated. A portable stool is used for this purpose.

Legs are retained by tightening a wing nut which exerts a clamping action.

Height adjustment is made by turning a knurled bolt head .79 inches (20 mm) in diameter. The pointed end of the bolt engages holes in a telescoping support shaft. The seat is placed over the end of the support shaft and revolves freely.

H. Drum sticks

The trap set is played with sticks, usually wooden, which are available in a wide variety of sizes. Length, diameter, and shape of striking end (head) of stick affect the sound of the instrument, and the selection of an appropriate size is a musical as well as physical consideration.

I. Assembly and Disassembly

Assembly and disassembly requirements involve manipulation of all holders. Assembly, disassembly, or adjustment of various components involves the manipulation of the mechanical attachments mentioned in the description of individual instruments.

II. Tuning Requirements

A. Cymbals

None

B. Bass drum

The bass drum is tuned by turning the tension rods which are located around the circumference of each drum head. Each of these rods has a T-shaped handle which is 2.36 inches (60 mm) long and is turned in a clockwise or counterclockwise direction against resistance. There are 10 of these handles on each side of the bass drum.

C. Mounted tom-tom and floor tom-tom

Both these drums are tuned with the use of a tuning key. The key is placed over the end of each tension rod and turned in a clockwise or counterclockwise direction against resistance. There are 6 tension rods located on each side of each drum.

These drums are also equipped with internal tone controls (muffler). Turning a knob .98 inches (25 mm) in diameter forces a felt pad into contact with the drum head and thus alters the tone.

D. Snare Drum

The snare drum heads are tensioned in the same manner as the tom-tom. There are tuning rods for each head and an internal tone control is present. The snares are coiled wires or pieces of nylon or gut which are held in contact with the bottom head of the drum. The snare strainer is located on the side of the drum and applies tension to the snare strands. Two adjustment devices are present. The first is a lever which, when pushed or pulled, releases the snares from contact with the bottom head and gives the drum a tom-tom sound. The second adjustment is a knob .59 inches (15 mm) in diameter, which increases or diminishes the amount of tension on the snares. These adjustments may be used frequently and operate against some resistance.

III. Transport

Transport involves disassembly of all components. Cases are not provided with the instrument but are available.

IV. Student Maintenance

A. Tuning

Drums must be tuned occasionally but certainly not with the frequency of woodwind, string or brass instruments.

B. Replacement of heads

Heads deteriorate with age and break. They may also break owing to improper tuning or overly energetic playing. The mounted tom-tom heads are particularly susceptible to breakage if placed at too great an angle. Replacement of heads involves the removal of all tension rods, lifting off the rim or counterhoop (metal ring around circumference of the drum and retaining the head), lifting off the damaged head, and setting a new one in position. The rim and rods are then replaced and the drum is tuned.

The bottom head (snare head) of the snare drum is easily damaged through improper positioning on its stand and is somewhat more complicated. Besides the removal of rim and rods, the snares themselves must be removed by loosening two small screws which hold them to the strainer mechanism.

V. Variation Among Manufacturers

A. Drum sizes

Note: First number indicates distance between heads. Second figure indicates head diameter.

Bass drum-14 x 18 inches (355.6 mm x 457.2 mm) to
16 x 26 inches (406.4 mm x 660.4 mm)
Mounted tom-tom-5-1/2 x 6 inches (139.7 mm x 152.4 mm)
to 15 x 16 inches (381 mm x 406.4 mm)
Floor tom-tom-14 x 14 inches (355.6 mm x 355.6 mm) to
18 x 20 inches (457.2 mm x 508 mm)
Snare drum-3 x 13 inches (76.2 mm x 330.2 mm) to
8 x 15 inches (203.2 mm x 381 mm)

B. Cymbals

Ride cymbals (diameter)-16 inches (406.4 mm) to
24 inches (609.6 mm)
Note: Smaller sizes, down to 10 inches, are available, but these should be considered inadequate for trap set use. Larger sizes, up to 30 inches, are also available but are difficult to obtain and expensive.
Hi-hat cymbals-12 inches (304.8 mm) to
15 inches (381 mm)

C. Hardware

Bass drum pedal

Pedals are available which allow a large number of adjustments, including length of pedal, angle of pedal to drum, pedal height, spring pressure beater height, and beater angle.

Hi-hat stands

Hi-stands are basically similar to model discussed.

Snare drum

Many stands do not exert a clamping action on the snare drum. These stands are somewhat easier to erect.

Cymbal stands

Stands may reach 59.06 inches (1500 mm) when fully extended. Boom stands may be erected to 66.93 inches (1700 mm), and an additional arm will move the cymbal 11.81 inches (300 mm) closer to the player over any obstructions. Cymbals may also be mounted directly on the bass drum.

Tom-tom holder

Tom-tom may be mounted on a separate stand. Each manufacturer has his own type of mechanism for mounting tom-tom to the brass drum.

Drum stools

Stools are basically similar to the model examined.

Instrument: Trap Set

Checklist

The following skills are necessary for independence in playing, owning, and receiving instruction on this instrument. The music teacher should confirm the need for those items, such as need for transport, which may not be necessary in all situations. The teacher should also add any items, such as the need to transport instructional materials to and from lessons, which may be applicable.

The therapist should indicate those requirements which a student is able to fulfill. The teacher or parents must provide for assistance in those areas in which a student may be dependent.

	Needed	Can Perform	Can Not Perform
1. Tune instrument	———	———	———
2. Transport instrument	———	———	———
3. Adjust position of instrument	———	———	———
4. Assemble instrument	———	———	———
5. Disassemble instrument	———	———	———
6. Remove and replace damaged heads	———	———	———
7. Place sticks in hands	———	———	———
8. Change sticks if necessary	———	———	———
9. Retrieve dropped sticks	———	———	———

TRAP SET

Considerations:
- General Body Position
- Major Body Parts Involved in Playing - Mobile/Stable Components - Functions of Major/Minor Joints Involved - Mobile/ Stable Capacity

The trap set is played in a manner requiring support *(stability)* and movement *(mobility)* of trunk, upper extremities, and lower extremities. The major individual joints required to function in a stable capacity are those of the trunk and hands. Movement is of major importance in the joints of the shoulder, elbows, wrists, and ankles.

Considerations:
- Major Muscle Groups
- Movement Observed

The trap set utilizes muscle groups to produce stability, rotation, flexion, abduction, and pronation/supination of both upper extremities. Wrist movements (one technique) include a rotary synergy of flexion/extension and deviation. Hands are held in a flexed position while holding sticks (right palm down, left thumb up). Trunk movement is rotation and flexion. Ankle movement produced is plantar/dorsiflexion. The degree of movement is greatest for shoulders, elbows, and wrists. Movement is used to a lesser degree in trunk and ankles.

Considerations:
- Muscle Strength
- Speed/Dexterity

Muscle strength utilized bilaterally in playing the trap set requires holding drum sticks up against gravity (Fair+ muscle grade) while moving in various directions for periods of time. Additional strength is required for drumming techniques using repeated arm movements (Good- to Good muscle grade). Lower extremity use for playing bass drum and hi-hat cymbal requires strength to overcome gravity (Fair+ to Good- muscle grade). The speed/dexterity utilized in arm movements is a very fine motor control requiring rapid, repetitive alternating movements, increasing with advanced playing.

Considerations:
- Sensation
- Perception

Playing the trap set appears to utilize the deep sensations for arm movements. Perceptual components appear to be in the areas of orientation, visual, and motor. Orientation mechanisms direct body movements using visual cues in a planned, coordinated manner. A high degree of perceptual skills is employed.

Considerations:
- Respiration
- Cardiac Output

The playing of the trap set requires moderate exertion (light work), which may increase with prolonged playing. Respiration must be adequate to maintain level of exertion without signs of fatigue.

Considerations:
- Vision
- Audition

The trap set appears to rely on visual skills, with most functional levels from normal to moderate low vision. Auditory levels most functional are in the normal to moderate impairment range.

TRAP SET

MAJOR MUSCLE GROUPS USED IN PLAYING
WITHOUT SUBSTITUTION OR ADAPTATION

KEY: B=Beginning Level
I =Intermediate Level
A=Advanced Level

P=Held Position for Playing
X=Muscle Movement Used in Playing
● =Increased Usage

Body Part	Function	Muscle or Muscle Groups	Left B	Left I	Left A	Right B	Right I	Right A
Scapula	Elevation	Trapezius (Inferior)	x	—	—	x	—	—
Shoulder	Flexion	Deltoideus (Anterior)	x	●	●	x	●	●
	Abduction	Deltoideus (Middle)	x	●	●	x	●	●
	External Rotation	External Rotator Group	x	●	●	x	●	●
	Internal Rotation	Internal Rotator Group	x	●	●	x	●	●
Elbow	Flexion	Biceps Brachii	x	—	—	x	—	—
		Brachialis						
Forearm	Supination	Supinator Group	x	●	●	x	●	●
	Pronation	Pronator Group	x	●	●	x	●	●
Wrist	Deviation, Radial	Flexor Carpi Radial.	x	—	—	x	—	—
		Extensor Carpi Rad. Longus						
		Extensor Carpi Rad. Brevis						
	Deviation, Ulnar	Flexor Carpi Ulnaris	x	—	—	x	—	—
		Extensor Carpi Ulnaris						
	Extension	Extensor Carpi Rad. Longus & Brevis	x	—	—	x	—	—
		Extensor Carpi Ulnaris						
	Flexion	Flexor Carpi Radial.	x	—	—	x	—	—
		Flexor Carpi Ulnaris						

Body Part	Function	Muscle or Muscle Groups	Left B	Left I	Left A	Right B	Right I	Right A
Fingers	MP Flexion	Lumbricales	p	—	—	p	—	—
	IP Flexion (1st)	Flex. Digit. Superior	p	—	—	p	—	—
	IP Flexion (2nd)	Flex. Digit. Prof.	p	—	—	p	—	—
	Adduction	Interossei Palmares	p	—	—	p	—	—
Thumb	Abduction	Abd. Poll. Longus	p	—	—	p	—	—
Trunk	Rotation	Obl. Ext. Abdominis						
		Obl. Int. Abdominis	x	—	—	x	—	—
	Extension	Thoracic Groups						
		Lumbar Group	x	—	—	x	—	—
Knee	Flexion	Biceps Femoris						
		Inner Hamstrings	p	—	—	p	—	—
Ankle	Dorsiflexion	Tibialis Anterior	x	—	—	x	—	—
	Plantar Flexion	Gastrocnemius						
		Soleus	x	—	—	x	—	—
Hip	Flexion	Iliopsoas	p	—	—	p	—	—

Muscles listed are used in the playing of this instrument; those not listed are not directly involved.

Facial and neck musculature is marked on right and left for convenience.
Increases (•) are noted in Intermediate Level and Advanced Level that are most obvious.
Muscles are used in groups for synergist movements rather than as isolated muscle movements.
Generally, X's in Beginning Level continue in Intermediate and Advanced Levels.

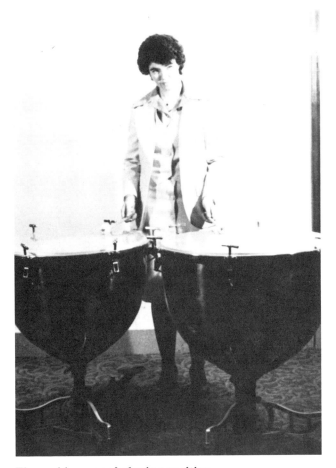

Timpani in normal playing position

Timpani foot pedal position

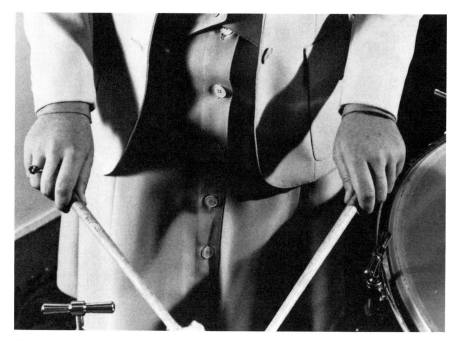

Timpani mallet position (for strokes)

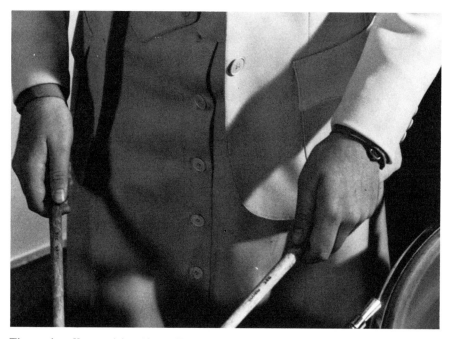

Timpani mallet position (for roll)

TRAP SET

MOVEMENT OBSERVED IN PLAYING
(ACTIVE & POSITIONAL)
WITHOUT SUBSTITUTION OR ADAPTATION*

These ranges were determined through working with musicians. They reflect the musician's body size, individuality, and possibly style. The ranges are approximate to give a working baseline for instrument suitability.

Note: Method used was one stick held palm down on right, and one stick held palm upward on left.

Head:		Neutral.
Shoulders:		Flex (40-60°) with abduction (0-40°) and internal rotation (–30-40°).
Elbows:		Flex (80-110°).
Forearms:	Left	Pronates (0-30°).
	Right	Pronates (0-40°) and supinates (0-40°).
Wrists:		Held in neutral with alternating use of ulnar and radial deviation (0-10°).
Thumbs:		Abducted and held opposite index finger.
Fingers:	Left	Flexed around stick in fist fashion with MP (60°), PIP (90°), DIP (60°).
	Right	Flexed around stick in a pronated prehension (tripod) position with MP (40°), PIP (40°), DIP (10°).

*I.e., using normal body position for playing, without any devices for instrument or body parts.

FAMILY: Percussion
INSTRUMENT: Timpani
TYPE: Pedal
MAKE: Slingerland
MODEL: Grand Pedal

Note: Timpani are usually arranged in pairs, although groups of three or four are not uncommon. The number of drums that a student would be working with will have a direct bearing on the range of motion needed for play. The following diagram indicates, from above, the usual arrangement of four timpani.

Distance between playing surfaces

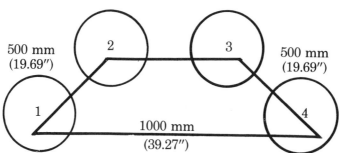

I. Assembly and Disassembly
    The timpani are not assembled or disassembled by the student.

II. Tuning Requirements
    These timpani are known as pedal timpani because of their tuning mechanism. Raising or lowering the pedal located on each drum adjusts the amount of tension in the playing surface (head) and thus causes a change in pitch. The range of pitches available is determined by the size of the drum. The pedal clutch mechanism must be unlocked before adjusting tension. The player rocks his foot toward the forward (toe) end of the pedal to release the clutch, adjusts the pedal height, and then rocks the nearest (heel) end of the pedal to lock it into the desired position. Considerable pressure must be exerted on the pedal during this operation. Tuning is often necessary during performance. While tuning, the player must tap the drum to test the accuracy of intonation in such a way that the music of a performing ensemble is not disturbed. This is usually accomplished by bending over the drum and placing the ear in close proximity to the head while retuning.
    The timpani are also equipped with rods which, when turned, vary the amount of tension placed on the head. These rods end in large T-shaped handles (tuning handles), 3.15 inches (80 mm) long by .51 inches (13 mm) in diameter located around the circumference of the head. These handles are turned in a clockwise or counterclockwise direction against resistance and are used for the initial tuning of a drum.
    Note: A timpani which has a playing surface (head) made of plastic (mylar) is stable, once tuned. Drums equipped with skin (calf or goat) playing heads respond to changes in temperature and humidity. Frequent readjustment is necessary.

III. Transport
    The timpani may need to be moved from room to room within a school or adjusted for position. Two legs on the tripod base of these timpani have casters. The third leg must be raised above the floor. The student must support a minimum of 13.61 kg (30 lb) to move the drum.

IV. Student Maintenance
    Because of the mechanical nature of the tuning mechanisms, student adjustments of pedals or replacement of heads is not advised.

V. Variations Among Manufacturers
   A. Pedal timpani
      1. Physical dimensions
         Physical dimensions are similar to those of the timpani examined.
      2. Pedal types
         Many timpani have pedals which do not require the locking and unlocking of a clutch mechanism. These pedals are moved with pressure from the toe or heel. Some of these models do not have the T-shaped rods used for initial tuning; a special wrench (tuning key) is used for these instruments.
   B. Timpani may be encountered which are not tuned by pedals. These types are as follows:
      1. Tuning handles-these drums must be tuned and retuned exclusively through the turning of T-shaped handles located around the circumference of the drum head.
      2. Single tuning handles-a single tuning handle is turned by the player. It is connected to other rods by linkage. All rods move simultaneously.
      3. Tuning cranks-a special wrench (crank) is placed over a single rod and turned. The head is uniformly tensioned by all rods simultaneously.
   C. During the last few years several types of timpani have been widely distributed. These instruments have been designed for elementary classroom or marching band use and may be found in many schools.
      1. Classroom timpani-these drums are small with diameters of approximately 300 mm to 500 mm (11.81 to 19.68 inches) and stand 600 mm to 900 mm (23.62 to 35.43 inches) above the floor. They may be cylindrical or parabolic (bowl) in overall shape. These drums, which are small timpani, are not adequate for use within a band or orchestra.
      2. Marching timpani-these drums are made to be carried and may weigh no more than 10 kg (22.05 lb). Available diameters are in the range of 500 mm to 750 mm (19.69 to 32 inches). Their chief advantage is that the legs telescope into the bowl and the playing surface can be brought to within 600 mm to 812.8 mm (23.62 to 27.56 inches) from the floor. Tuning mechanisms are generally crank type.

VI. Other Devices
   A. Many timpani are equipped with tuning gauges. These gauges, once calibrated, react to playing head travel and indicate at what point a specific pitch will be produced.
   B. The timpani may be played from a seated position. A portable drum stool is generally used for this purpose. Such stools are adjustable in height from 500 mm to 700 mm (19.68 to 27.65 inches) and have seat diameters of 280 mm (11.02 inches).

Checklist

The following skills are necessary for independence in playing, owning, and receiving instruction on this instrument. The music teacher should confirm the need for those items, such as need for transport, which may not be necessary in all situations. The teacher should also add any items, such as the need to transport instructional materials to and from lessons, which may be applicable.

The therapist should indicate those requirements which a student is able to fulfill. The teacher or parents must provide for assistance in those areas in which a student may be dependent.

	Needed	Can Perform	Can Not Perform
1. Reach between two drums	_____	_____	_____
2. Reach between three drums	_____	_____	_____
3. Reach between four drums	_____	_____	_____
4. Place mallets in hands	_____	_____	_____
5. Retrieve dropped mallets	_____	_____	_____
6. Change mallets if necessary	_____	_____	_____
7. Manipulate tuning handles	_____	_____	_____
8. Depress or raise pedal	_____	_____	_____
9. Adjust position of instrument	_____	_____	_____
10. Move instrument from place to place within a school	_____	_____	_____
11. Adjust stool	_____	_____	_____

TIMPANI

Considerations:
- General Body Position
- Major Body Parts Involved in Playing - Mobile/Stable Components - Functions of Major/Minor Joints Involved - Mobile/Stable Capacity

The timpani is played in a manner requiring support *(stability)* and movement *(mobility)* of trunk, upper extremities, and lower extremity (pedal). The major individual joints required to function in a stable capacity are those of the hands. Movement is of major importance in shoulders, elbows, and wrists bilaterally.

Considerations:
- Major Muscle Groups
- Movement Observed

The timpani utilizes muscle groups to produce stabilization, flexion, abduction, rotation, and pronation/supination of both upper extremities. Wrists are held in extension with combined movements of deviation and pronation/supination. Fingers are flexed around beater in a pronated fashion. The degree of movement is greatest for the shoulders and forearms bilaterally. Movement is used to a lesser degree in elbows and trunk rotation.

Considerations:
- Muscle Strength
- Speed/Dexterity

Muscle strength utilized bilaterally in playing the timpani requires holding arms and beater up against gravity (Fair+ muscle grade) for periods of time. Additional strength is required to strike drums (Good- to Good muscle grade) and particularly for accentuation. Lower extremity strength requirement is raising foot against gravity to depress pedal (Good muscle grade). Dexterity requirement is one of fine extremity adjustment.

Considerations:
- Sensation
- Perception

Playing the timpani appears to utilize the deep sensations for arm movements. Perceptual components appear to be in the areas of orientation, visual, and motor. (Exclude visual for non-sighted individuals.) Orientation mechanisms direct body movements, using visual cues in a planned coordinated manner.

Considerations:
- Respiration
- Cardiac Output

The playing of the timpani requires moderate exertion (light work). Respiration must be adequate to maintain level of exertion without fatigue.

Considerations:
- Vision
- Audition

The timpani can be played by sighted individuals and also by those at any level of visual impairment. (Tactile/kinesthetic modalities may be primarily relied upon). Auditory levels most functional are in the range of normal to moderate impairment.

TIMPANI

MAJOR MUSCLE GROUPS USED IN PLAYING WITHOUT SUBSTITUTION OR ADAPTATION

KEY:
B=Beginning Level
I =Intermediate Level
A=Advanced Level

P=Held Position for Playing
X=Muscle Movement Used in Playing
•=Increased Usage

Body Part	Function	Muscle or Muscle Groups	Left B	Left I	Left A	Right B	Right I	Right A
Scapula	Stabilization	Serratus Anterior	x	—	—		—	—
	Abduction	Trapezius (Superior)						
	Elevation	Trapezius (Inferior)				x	—	—
	Depression	Trapezius (Middle)						
	Adduction	Rhomboideus Major & Minor						
Shoulder	Flexion	Deltoideus (Anterior)	x	—	—	x	—	—
	Abduction	Deltoideus (Middle)	x	—	—	x	—	—
	External Rotation	External Rotator Group	x	—	—	x	—	—
	Internal Rotation	Internal Rotator Group	x	—	—	x	—	—
Elbow	Flexion	Biceps Brachii	x	—	—	x	—	—
		Brachialis						
Forearm	Supination	Supinator Group	x	—	—	x	—	—
	Pronation	Pronator Group	x	—	—	x	—	—
Wrist	Deviation, Radial	Flexor Carpi Radial.	x	—	—		—	—
		Extensor Carpi Rad. Longus				x	—	—
		Extensor Carpi Rad. Brevis						
	Deviation, Ulnar	Flexor Carpi Ulnaris	x	—	—		—	—
		Extensor Carpi Ulnaris				x	—	—

Body Part	Function	Muscle or Muscle Groups	Left B	Left I	Left A	Right B	Right I	Right A
	Extension	Extensor Carpi Rad. Longus & Brevis	x			x		
		Extensor Carpi Ulnaris						
	Flexion	Flexor Carpi Radial.	x			x		
		Flexor Carpi Ulnaris						
Fingers	MP Flexion	Lumbricales	p			p		
	IP Flexion (1st)	Flex. Digit. Superior	p			p		
	IP Flexion (2nd)	Flex. Digit. Prof.	p			p		
	MP Extension	Ext. Digit. Com.						
	Adduction	Interossei Palmares	p			p		
Thumb	Adduction	Add. Poll.	p			p		
	Opposition							
Trunk	Rotation	Obl. Ext. Abdominis	x	•	•	x	•	•
		Obl. Int. Abdominis		•	•		•	•
Hip	Flexion	Iliopsoas			x			
	Extension	Gluteus Maximus						x
Knee	Flexion	Biceps Femoris			x			
		Inner Hamstrings						x
Ankle	Dorsiflexion	Tibialis Anterior			x			x
	Plantar Flexion	Gastrocnemius						
		Soleus			x			x

Muscles listed are used in the playing of this instrument; those not listed are not directly involved.

Facial and neck musculature is marked on right and left for convenience.
Increases (•) are noted in Intermediate Level and Advanced Level that are most obvious.
Muscles are used in groups for synergist movements rather than as isolated muscle movements.
Generally, X's in Beginning Level continue in Intermediate and Advanced Levels.

TIMPANI

MOVEMENT OBSERVED IN PLAYING
(ACTIVE & POSITIONAL)
WITHOUT SUBSTITUTION OR ADAPTATION*

These ranges were determined through working with musicians. They reflect the musician's body size, individuality, and possibly style. The ranges are approximate to give a working baseline for instrument suitability.

Head: Neutral position.

Shoulders: Flexes (20- -20°) with abduction (50°), internal rotation (0-60°), and trunk rotation from drum to drum.

Elbows: Flex (70-90°) with shoulder, abducted and internally rotated.

Forearms: Pronated (20- -60°) with deviation.

Wrists: Extended (20°) with full range of ulnar deviation when striking, and slight radial deviation on upward return.

Thumbs: Abducted and flexed around sticks.

Fingers: Flexed and adducted around sticks. MP full range, PIP full range, and DIP full range.

Lower Extremities: The leg may be required to flex at hip, knee, and ankle for pedal in advanced playing.

*I.e., using normal body position for playing, without any devices for instrument or body parts.

Marimba in normal playing position

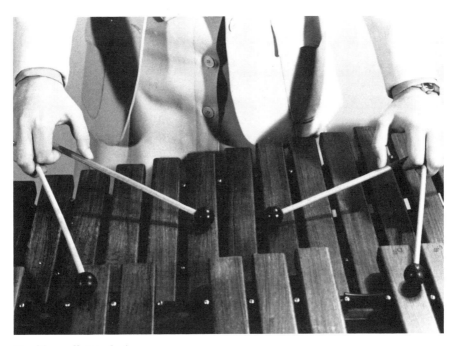

Double mallet technique

Single mallet technique

FAMILY: Percussion
INSTRUMENT: Xylophone
TYPE: 4 Octave
MAKE: Deagan
MODEL: No model specifications
MATERIALS USED IN CONSTRUCTION: Wooden Bars

I. Assembly and Disassembly
The xylophone is not assembled or disassembled by the student. It is possible on some models to fold the legs and remove the resonating tubes if transport is necessary.

II. Tuning Requirements
The xylophone is not tuned by the student and must usually be returned to the manufacturer if such service is necessary.

III. Transport
The instrument examined is not supplied with a case since transport is not usual when traveling to lessons. It may be necessary to move the instrument from room to room within a school and the instrument is supplied with casters for this purpose.

IV. Student Maintenance
None.

V. Variation Among Manufacturers
Length of keyboard may vary considerably owing to the addition or deletion of various notes rather than the width of individual bars. Bars on many instruments may vary in width, with the widest bar found in the lowest range.

Instrument: Xylophone

Checklist

The following skills are necessary for independence in playing, owning, and receiving instruction on this instrument. The music teacher should confirm the need for those items, such as need for transport, which may not be necessary in all situations. The teacher should also add any items, such as the need to transport instructional materials to and from lessons, which may be applicable.

The therapist should indicate those requirements which a student is able to fulfill. The teacher or parents must provide for assistance in those areas in which a student may be dependent.

	Needed	Can Perform	Can Not Perform
1. Place mallets in hands	_____	_____	_____
2. Change mallets if necessary	_____	_____	_____
3. Adjust position of instrument	_____	_____	_____
4. Transport instrument from place to place within a school	_____	_____	_____

FAMILY: Percussion
INSTRUMENT: Marimba*
TYPE: 2-1/2 Octaves
MAKE: Jen-Co
MODEL: Not Specified
MATERIALS USED IN CONSTRUCTION: Wooden Bars

I.   Assembly and Disassembly
     The marimba is not assembled or disassembled by the student. It is possible on some models to fold the legs and remove the resonating tubes if transport is necessary.

II.   Tuning Requirements
     The marimba is not tuned by the student and must usually be returned to the manufacturer if such service is necessary.

III.   Transport
     The instrument examined is not supplied with a case since transport is not usual when traveling to lessons. However, legs can be folded beneath the instrument after resonators have been removed. A handle is provided. It may be necessary to transport the instrument from room to room within a school and casters are provided for this purpose.

IV.   Student Maintenance
     None.

V.   Variation Among Manufacturers
     Length of keyboard may vary considerably owing to the addition or deletion of various notes rather than the width of individual bars. Bars on many instruments may vary in width, with the widest bars found in the lowest range.

*See pictures of xylophone for hand positions.

Instrument: Marimba

Checklist

The following skills are necessary for independence in playing, owning, and receiving instruction on this instrument. The music teacher should confirm the need for those items, such as need for transport, which may not be necessary in all situations. The teacher should also add any items, such as the need to transport instructional materials to and from lessons, which may be applicable.

The therapist should indicate those requirements which a student is able to fulfill. The teacher or parents must provide for assistance in those areas in which a student may be dependent.

	Needed	Can Perform	Can Not Perform
1. Place mallets in hands	_____	_____	_____
2. Change mallets if necessary	_____	_____	_____
3. Adjust position of instrument	_____	_____	_____
4. Transport instrument from place to place within a school	_____	_____	_____

FAMILY: Percussion
INSTRUMENT: Vibraphone*
TYPE: 3 Octave
MAKE: Ludwig/Musser
MODEL: One Nighter
MATERIALS USED IN CONSTRUCTION: Metal Bars

Note: Instrument must be connected to AC power supply. Electrical controls (2) are located beneath keyboard at player's right hand. Controls consist of one toggle switch (on-off) and one dial (adjust motor speed).

I.   Assembly and Disassembly
The vibraphone is not assembled or disassembled by the student. It is possible on some models to fold the legs and remove resonator if transport is necessary.

II.   Tuning Requirements
The vibraphone is not tuned by the student and must usually be returned to the manufacturer if such service is necessary.

III.   Transport
The instrument examined is not supplied with a case. Transport is not usual when traveling to and from lessons, although cases are available. It may be necessary to move the instrument from room to room within a school and casters are provided for this purpose.

IV.   Student Maintenance
None.

V.   Variation Among Manufacturers
Length of keyboard may vary considerably owing to the addition of various notes rather than the width of individual bars. Bars on many instruments may vary in width, with the widest bar found in the lowest range.

*See pictures of xylophone for hand positions.

Checklist

The following skills are necessary for independence in playing, owning, and receiving instruction on this instrument. The music teacher should confirm the need for those items, such as need for transport, which may not be necessary in all situations. The teacher should also add any items, such as the need to transport instructional materials to and from lessons, which may be applicable.

The therapist should indicate those requirements which a student is able to fulfill. The teacher or parents must provide for assistance in those areas in which a student may be dependent.

	Needed	Can Perform	Can Not Perform
1. Place mallets in hands	_____	_____	_____
2. Change mallets if necessary	_____	_____	_____
3. Adjust position of instrument	_____	_____	_____
4. Transport instrument from place to place within a school	_____	_____	_____
5. Connect instrument to AC power supply	_____	_____	_____
6. Turn power supply on and off	_____	_____	_____
7. Adjust motor speed	_____	_____	_____

XYLOPHONE - 3 Octave
MARIMBA - 3 Octave
VIBRAPHONE - 2-1/2 Octave

These three instruments are considered together, as the same basic components are used in playing each of them. Differences are described in individual sections.

Considerations:
- General Body Position
- Major Body Parts Involved in Playing - Mobile/Stable Components - Functions of Major/Minor Joints Involved - Mobile/Stable Capacity

These instruments are played in a manner requiring support *(stability)* and movement *(mobility)* of trunk and upper extremities. The vibraphone, in addition, requires stability and mobility of the lower extremities. The major individual joints required to function in a stable capacity are those of the right and left hands. (Stability of the lower extremities is implied, as instruments are normally played in a standing position.) Movement is of major importance in joints of the shoulders, elbows and wrists. Movement of the lower extremity is noted at ankle in vibraphone only for depressing pedal.

Considerations:
- Major Muscle Groups
- Movement Observed

These instruments utilize muscle groups to produce stability, flexion, abduction, rotation, and pronation of upper extremities. Wrists are extended with fingers flexed around beaters. The trunk is rotated as range of instruments is used. Ankle is flexed in vibraphone for depressing pedal. The degree of movement is greatest for shoulders and elbows. Movement is used to a lesser degree for trunk rotation and in wrists.

Considerations:
- Muscle Strength
- Speed/Dexterity

Muscle strength utilized bilaterally in playing the instruments requires holding the sticks up against gravity (Fair+ muscle grade) for periods of time. Additional strength is required for striking notes (Good- muscle grade), increasing with playing time. The speed/dexterity in playing the instruments requires fine movements of arms and wrists in rapidly alternating patterns.

Considerations:
- Sensation
- Perception

Playing these instruments appears to utilize the deep sensations for arm movements and proper striking technique. Perceptual components appear to be in the areas of orientation, visual, and motor. Orientation mechanisms direct body movements using visual cues in a planned, coordinated manner. A high degree of perceptual skills is employed, and individuals lacking visual skills or acuity may encounter great difficulties with initial playing.

Considerations:
- Respiration
- Cardiac Output

The playing of these instruments requires moderate exertion (light work) which may increase with prolonged playing time. Respiration must be adequate to maintain level of exertion without signs of fatigue.

Considerations:
- Vision
- Audition

The instruments appear to rely on vision, with most functional levels from normal to moderately low vision. Auditory levels most functional are in the normal to moderate impairment range.

XYLOPHONE - MARIMBA - VIBRAPHONE

MAJOR MUSCLE GROUPS USED IN PLAYING
WITHOUT SUBSTITUTION OR ADAPTATION

KEY: B=Beginning Level
      I =Intermediate Level
      A=Advanced Level

P=Held Position for Playing
X=Muscle Movement Used in Playing
• =Increased Usage

Body Part	Function	Muscle or Muscle Groups	Left B	Left I	Left A	Right B	Right I	Right A
Scapula	Elevation	Trapezius (Inferior)	x	—	—	x	—	—
Shoulder	Flexion	Deltoideus (Anterior)	x	•	•	x	•	•
	Abduction	Deltoideus (Middle)	x	•	•	x	•	•
	External Rotation	External Rotator Group	x	—	—	x	—	—
	Internal Rotation	Internal Rotator Group	x	—	—	x	—	—
Elbow	Flexion	Biceps Brachii / Brachialis	x	•	•	x	•	•
Forearm	Supination	Supinator Group	x	•	•	x	•	•
	Pronation	Pronator Group	x	•	•	x	•	•
Wrist	Deviation, Ulnar	Flexor Carpi Ulnaris / Extensor Carpi Ulnaris	x	•	•	x	•	•
	Extension	Extensor Carpi Rad. Longus & Brevis / Extensor Carpi Ulnaris	x	•	•	x	•	•
	Flexion	Flexor Carpi Radial. / Flexor Carpi Ulnaris	x	•	•	x	•	•

Body Part	Function	Muscle or Muscle Groups	Left B	Left I	Left A	Right B	Right I	Right A
Fingers	MP Flexion	Lumbricales	p			p		
	IP Flexion (1st)	Flex. Digit. Superior	p			p		
	Adduction	Interossei Palmares	p			p		
Thumb	MP Flexion	Flex. Poll. Brevis	p			p		
	IP Flexion	Flex. Poll. Longus	p			p		
Trunk	Rotation	Obl. Ext. Abdominis		x			x	
		Obl. Int. Abdominis			•			•
Ankle*	Dorsiflexion	Tibialis Anterior	x			x		
		Gastrocnemius						
	Plantar Flexion	Soleus	x			x		

*Vibraphone only

Muscles listed are used in the playing of this instrument; those not listed are not directly involved.

Facial and neck musculature is marked on right and left for convenience.
Increases (•) are noted in Intermediate Level and Advanced Level that are most obvious.
Muscles are used in groups for synergist movements rather than as isolated muscle movements.
Generally, X's in Beginning Level continue in Intermediate and Advanced Levels.

XYLOPHONE - MARIMBA - VIBRAPHONE

MOVEMENT OBSERVED IN PLAYING
(ACTIVE & POSITIONAL)
WITHOUT SUBSTITUTION OR ADAPTATION*

These ranges were determined through working with musicians. They reflect the musician's body size, individuality, and possibly style. The ranges are approximate to give a working baseline for instrument suitability.

Head:	Held in neutral position.
Shoulders:	Flexes (-20 -30°) with abduction (30-60°) and internal rotation (20-60°). Abduction increases as range increases.
Elbows:	Flex (60-75°) with shoulder abduction and rotation.
Forearms:	Pronates (60-90°), increasing as note is struck.
Wrists:	Extends (30-35°) with sticks held in slight ulnar deviation.
Thumbs:	Abducted to index finger as in a fisted fashion around mallet handle.
Fingers:	Flexed in fist fashion: MP (75°), PIP (100°), DIP (90°).
Trunk:	Rotates from side to side as range of keys used increases.
Ankles:	Flexes to hold bar down (vibraphone only) during play.

*I.e., using normal body position for playing, without any devices for instrument or body parts.

Piano in normal playing position

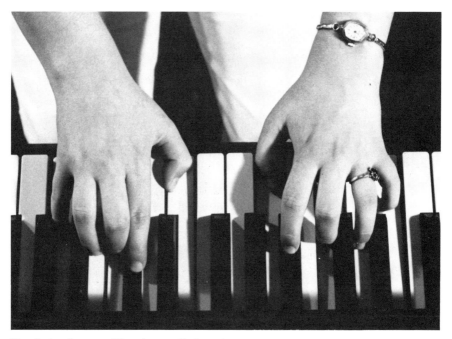

Hands in close position (normal), top view

Piano, hands apart (extreme playing position)

Hands apart position, Piano, top view

FAMILY: KEYBOARD

INSTRUMENTS: ACOUSTIC PIANO

                ELECTRIC PIANO

FAMILY: Keyboard
INSTRUMENTS: Acoustic Piano and Electric Piano

The piano is unique among the instruments examined in that it is the only instrument in which all fingers can be used to produce simultaneous notes of varying pitch. It is often considered a percussion instrument (although not by percussionists or pianists) since the interior strings are struck by felt-headed hammers. The typewriter and piano are sometimes considered mechanically similar, and while this analogy is not appreciated by pianists, it does possess a certain amount of validity; however, the genius of design in the piano action is not in the similar structure of levers and balances which raise the keys, but rather in the fact that, once the string is struck, the hammer is released and the string permitted to resonate in a manner that can be controlled somewhat by the player through the use of pedals.

The action of the electric piano examined was purposely designed to duplicate the standard piano mechanics and keyboard layout. There are hammers on the interior but they strike tuned metal rods, the sound of which is sensed by an electronic pickup which runs the length of the interior. It is actually the pickup which is then connected to an external amplifier via a cord. Some other makes of electric pianos are truly electronic in that the sound of the instrument is synthesized, that is, produced by the action of various devices on electrical current.

PIANO

INSTRUMENT SELECTION GUIDE

An "X" indicates a potential physical limitation in relationship to "normal" use of the instrument. The presence of an "X" should not necessarily preclude consideration of the instrument if compensatory techniques and adaptations are appropriate.

Potential Limitations		Comments
Contractures of		
Neck	X	If limits arm position and range requirement
Shoulders	X	If limits arm position and range requirement
Elbows	X	If limits arm position and range requirement
Wrists	X	If limits arm position and range requirement
Fingers	X	If limits range requirement
Hips	—	
Knees	—	
Ankles	X	If pedals used
Incoordination		
Gross - Upper Extremities	X	If moderate - severe
- Lower Extremities	X	If pedals used and moderate - severe
Fine - Upper Extremities	X	If moderate - severe
- Lower Extremities	—	
Limb Loss (prosthesis fit implied)		
- Upper Extremities		
- Above Elbow	X	Questionable
- Below Elbow	X	Questionable
- Partial Hand	X	Questionable
- Lower Extremities		
- Above Knee	X	If pedals cannot be used or adapted
- Below Knee	X	If pedals cannot be used or adapted
- Symes	X	If pedals cannot be used or adapted
- Partial Foot	X	If pedals cannot be used or adapted
- Hip Disarticulation	X	If pedals cannot be used or adapted

Potential Limitations

		Comments
Movement		
Athetoid	- Upper Extremities	If moderate - severe
	- Lower Extremities	If moderate - severe
Rigidity	- Upper Extremities	
	- Lower Extremities	
Fluctuating Tone	- Upper Extremities	If moderate - severe
	- Lower Extremities	
Tremor		
Resting	- Upper Extremities	If moderate - severe
Intention	- Upper Extremities	If moderate - severe
Dysmetria	- Upper Extremities	If moderate - severe
Pain		If limiting
Perception - Children		
	Apraxia	If moderate - severe
	Posture & Bilateral Integration	If moderate - severe
	Space Visual	If moderate - severe
Adults		
	Neglect	If uncompensated for
	Hemianopsia	If uncompensated for
	Spatial	If uncompensated for
	Apraxia	
Sensation		
	Tactile	If impaired or absent
	Proprioception	If impaired or absent
	Kinesthesia	If impaired or absent
Spasticity	- Upper Extremities	If mild to moderate - severe
	- Lower Extremities	If moderate - severe

Potential Limitations

		Comments
Weakness		
Proximal - Head/Neck		
- Shoulders	X	If limits playing position
- Trunk	X	If limits playing position
Distal - Upper Extremities	X	If below minimum requirement (F+)
- Lower Extremities	X	If pedals used

188

FAMILY: Keyboard
INSTRUMENT: Piano
TYPE: Acoustic
MAKE: Baldwin

I.   Assembly and Disassembly
     The piano does not require assembly or disassembly on the part of the student. It should be noted that the keyboard is provided with a wooden cover which protects the keyboard when not in use. This cover also prevents the accumulation of dust between keys, which eventually will adversely affect finely adjusted internal mechanisms, thus causing excessive wear. The piano examined in this instance required lifting of the cover, which weighs 2.5 kg (5.51 lb) through the use of two knobs 19 mm (.75 inch) in diameter and 1035 mm (40.75 inches) (center to center) apart. The entire lid is then pushed away from the player and slides into the body of the piano. The edge of this lid also serves as a support for printed music, which rests against a board provided for this purpose. The procedure is reversed for closing the cover. This mechanism varies from piano to piano and should be examined.

II. Tuning Requirements
     The piano is tuned by a highly skilled professional who also performs any other needed adjustments or repair.

III. Transport
     None.

IV. Student Maintenance
     None.

V.   Variation Among Manufacturers
     Some pianos may have two pedals instead of three.

Instrument: Acoustic Piano

Checklist

The following skills are necessary for independence in playing, owning, and receiving instruction on this instrument. The music teacher should confirm the need for those items, such as need for transport, which may not be necessary in all situations. The teacher should also add any items, such as the need to transport instructional materials to and from lessons, which may be applicable.

The therapist should indicate those requirements which a student is able to fulfill. The teacher or parents must provide for assistance in those areas in which a student may be dependent.

	Needed	Can Perform	Can Not Perform
1. Move keyboard cover	_____	_____	_____
2. Adjust stool or bench	_____	_____	_____

FAMILY: Keyboard
INSTRUMENT: Piano
TYPE: Electric Portable
MAKE: Fender/Rhodes
MODEL: 77

Note: Although some electric pianos are manufactured for stationary use, the vast majority of instruments are produced as portables. The data presented on this instrument reflects this latter method of construction. There is no reason why the instrument cannot be left standing for long periods of time as a stationary piano. Some inherent features, such as adjustable legs, compactness, availability of shorter keyboards, and volume control through the use of electronic means, may make the instrument appropriate for many individuals. However, the merits of acoustic versus electric piano must be decided by the type and style of music which is to be played.

The following data does not take the means of amplification into consideration since this is not a playing component of the instrument. It is, however, a necessary component if the instrument is to produce sound. The instrument is connected to the amplifier via a cord with phone type connectors. A socket and two tone controls are located above the keyboard on the left (facing keyboard). The amplifier need not be manipulated by the student during play except for turning it on and off. If manipulation of controls on the amplifier is desired, then available units should be examined in order to determine the student's ability to reach and adjust the individual controls. Many pedals are marketed which may enable the student to control tone through foot and ankle movement during play.

I.   Assembly and Disassembly
     If transport is necessary, the student must find some means of having the instrument weight supported while unscrewing the front legs of the instrument and loosening the clamps which retain the rear legs.

II. Tuning Requirements
     The piano may be tuned by the student and instructions are supplied with the instrument. This process involves removing the top of the instrument and turning small screws located near each sounding rod.

III. Transport
     The instrument must be disassembled for transport. Cases are not provided with the instrument and must be purchased as a separate item. Weight with cases will still equal 50 kg (110.23 lb.) for the largest component.

IV. Student Maintenance
     Electric pianos of this type tend to go out of tune, especially if subject to transport. The student may have difficulty obtaining a professional to perform this service.

V.   Variation Among Manufacturers
     Width of keys is standardized. Differences in length of keyboard should be attributed to addition or deletion of keys. Lighter (and heavier) units are available and should be examined if transport is a consideration. Some units may have self-contained amplification systems.

Checklist

The following skills are necessary for independence in playing, owning, and receiving instruction on this instrument. The music teacher should confirm the need for those items, such as need for transport, which may not be necessary in all situations. The teacher should also add any items, such as the need to transport instructional materials to and from lessons, which may be applicable.

The therapist should indicate those requirements which a student is able to fulfill. The teacher or parents must provide for assistance in those areas in which a student may be dependent.

	Needed	Can Perform	Can Not Perform
1. Adjust stool	————	————————	————
2. Connect instrument to amplifier	————	————————	————
3. Turn AC power on and off	————	————————	————
4. Turn control knobs on instrument	————	————————	————
5. Use pedal	————	————————	————

PIANO (88 Keys)
(Electric: 61 and 65 keys)

The standard piano and the electric piano are considered together, as the same basic components are used in playing. Differences are described in individual sections.

Considerations:
- General Body Position
- Major Body Parts Involved in Playing - Mobile/Stable Components - Functions of Major/Minor Joints Involved - Mobile/Stable Capacity

The piano is played in a manner requiring support *(stability)* and movement *(mobility)* of the trunk, upper extremities, and lower extremities (i.e., for pedals). The trunk functions as the major stabilizer. Movement is of major importance in shoulders, wrists, and hands.

Considerations:
- Major Muscle Groups
- Movement Observed

The piano utilizes muscle groups to produce stabilization, flexion, rotation, abduction, and pronation/supination of the upper extremities. Hand and wrist movements include flexion, extension, deviation, abduction, and adduction. Trunk rotation, flexion, and pelvic elevation are utilized when the full range of the keyboard is used. Little or no trunk rotation is utilized for the electric piano.

Ankle flexion is employed when pedals are required. The degree of movement is greatest in wrists and fingers. Movement is used to a lesser degree in trunk, shoulders, and elbows.

Considerations:
- Muscle Strength
- Speed/Dexterity

Muscle strength utilized bilaterally in playing the piano requires holding arms up against gravity (Fair+ muscle grade) for periods of time. Additional strength is required for repeated up/down finger movements and striking keys (Good- to Good muscle grade), increasing with playing time.

The electric piano requires only a light touch for striking keys, relying on less strength for play (Fair+ muscle grade). Strength for pedals requires foot raised against gravity (Fair+ muscle grade) and increases with prolonged playing (Good- to Good muscle grade).

The speed/dexterity of the hands for fingering relies on alternating, rolling, up/down movements with isolated, coupled, and mass execution.

Considerations:
- Sensation
- Perception

Playing the piano appears to utilize the deep sensations for arm movements and key depression. Perceptual components appear to be in the areas of orientation, visual, and motor. (Exclude visual for non-sighted individuals.) Orientation mechanisms direct body movements, using visual cues in a planned, coordinated manner.

Considerations:
- Respiration
- Cardiac Output

The playing of the piano requires moderate exertion (light work), which may increase with prolonged playing. Respiration must be adequate to maintain level of execution without signs of fatigue. It is believed that playing the electric piano is somewhat less demanding owing to decreased physical requirements needed to play.

Considerations:
- Vision
- Audition

The piano may be played by sighted individuals and also by those at any level of visual impairment. (Tactile/kinesthetic modalities may be primarily relied upon.) Auditory levels most functional are in the normal to moderate impairment range.

PIANO

MAJOR MUSCLE GROUPS USED IN PLAYING
WITHOUT SUBSTITUTION OR ADAPTATION

KEY: B=Beginning Level
       I =Intermediate Level
       A=Advanced Level

P=Held Position for Playing
X=Muscle Movement Used in Playing
• =Increased Usage

Body Part	Function	Muscle or Muscle Groups	Left B	Left I	Left A	Right B	Right I	Right A
Scapula	Stabilization	Serratus Anterior	x			x		
	Abduction	Trapezius (Superior)						
	Elevation	Trapezius (Inferior)						
	Depression	Trapezius (Middle)						
	Adduction	Rhomboideus Major & Minor						
Shoulder	Flexion	Deltoideus (Anterior)	x	•		x	•	•
	Abduction	Deltoideus (Middle)	x		•	x		•
	External Rotation	External Rotator Group	x			x		
	Internal Rotation	Internal Rotator Group	x			x		
Elbow	Flexion	Biceps Brachii	x	•		x	•	
		Brachialis						
Forearm	Supination	Supinator Group	x			x		
	Pronation	Pronator Group	x			x		
Wrist	Deviation, Radial	Flexor Carpi Radial.						
		Extensor Carpi Rad. Longus	x					
		Extensor Carpi Rad. Brevis				x		
	Deviation, Ulnar	Flexor Carpi Ulnaris	x					
		Extensor Carpi Ulnaris				x		
	Extension	Extensor Carpi Rad. Longus & Brevis						

Body Part	Function	Muscle or Muscle Groups	Left B	Left I	Left A	Right B	Right I	Right A
	Flexion	Extensor Carpi Ulnaris	x	—	—	x	—	—
		Flexor Carpi Radial.	x	—	—	x	—	—
		Flexor Carpi Ulnaris	x	—	—	x	—	—
Fingers	MP Flexion	Lumbricales	x	—	—	x	—	—
	IP Flexion (1st)	Flex. Digit. Superior	x	—	—	x	—	—
	IP Flexion (2nd)	Flex. Digit. Prof.	x	—	—	x	—	—
	MP Extension	Ext. Digit. Com.	x	—	—	x	—	—
	Adducti n	Interossei Palmares	x	—	—	x	—	—
	Abduction	Interossei Dorsales	x	—	—	x	—	—
		Abduct. Digit. Min.	x	—	—	x	—	—
Thumb	MP Flexion	Flex. Poll. Brevis	x	—	—	x	—	—
	IP Flexion	Flex. Poll. Longus	x	—	—	x	—	—
	MP Extension	Ext. Poll. Brevis	x	—	—	x	—	—
	IP Extension	Ext. Poll. Longus	x	—	—	x	—	—
	Abduction	Abd. Poll. Brevis						
		Abd. Poll. Longus	x	—	—	x	—	—
	Adduction	Add. Poll.	x	—	—	x	—	—
Trunk	Rotation	Obl. Ext. Abdominis						
		Obl. Int. Abdominis	—	x	•	—	x	•
	Extension	Thoracic Group	x	—	—	x	—	—
		Lumbar Group						
Hip	Pelvic Elevation	Quadratus Lumb.	x	x	•	x	x	•
	Flexion	Iliopsoas	p	—	—	p	—	—
Knee	Flexion	Biceps Femoris						
		Inner Hamstrings	p	—	—	p	—	—
Ankle	Dorsiflexion	Tibialis Anterior*	x	•	•	x	•	•
*Pedals								

Muscles listed are used in the playing of this instrument; those not listed are not directly involved.

Facial and neck musculature is marked on right and left for convenience.
Increases (•) are noted in Intermediate Level and Advanced Level that are most obvious.
Muscles are used in groups for synergist movements rather than as isolated muscle movements.
Generally, X's in Beginning Level continue in Intermediate and Advanced Levels.

PIANO

MOVEMENT OBSERVED IN PLAYING
(ACTIVE & POSITIONAL)
WITHOUT SUBSTITUTION OR ADAPTATION*

These ranges were determined through working with musicians. They reflect the musician's body size, individuality, and possibly style. The ranges are approximate to give a working baseline for instrument suitability.

Head:	Held in neutral position.
Shoulders:	Flex (0–40°) and abduction (20°), with play at center of keyboard. During increased range use, abduction increases (20–60°) on one side with adduction toward midline on the opposite side. Actions reverse as play moves on other side of keyboard.
Elbows:	Flex (80–95°) with shoulder movements.
Forearms:	Fully pronated with minor adjustments during play (0–10°).
Wrists:	Extend (0–20°) with ulnar and radial deviation used, (0–20°) as reach is extended and fingers abducted.
Thumbs:	Abduct (0–40°) and adduct to base of third finger.
Fingers:	Flex MP (0–60°), PIP (0–60°), DIP (20°), with abduction and adduction used during reach of keys.
Trunk:	Rotates as range of keyboard is used.
Electric Piano:	With decreased number of keys, a decrease of trunk rotation will be needed.
Ankles:	Flex (0–40°) with use of pedals.
Electric Piano:	Foot may be pressing pedal for periods of time due to nature of piano.

*I.e., using normal body position for playing, without any devices for instrument or body parts.

REFERENCES

1. Alvin, Julietta: Music for the Handicapped Child. Oxford University Press, 1965.
2. Angle, C.: Malocclusion of the Teeth, Ed. 7. Philadelphia, SS White Dental Mfg. Co., 1907.
3. Ayres, Jean: Sensory Integration and Learning Disorders. Western Psychological Services, 1972.
4. Banus, Barbara Sharpe: The Developmental Therapist. Charles B. Slack, Inc., 1971.
5. Barton, E.: Air Pressures Used in Playing Brass Instruments. Phil. Mag., 3:16, pp. 385-393, April 1902.
6. Boone, Daniel: The Voice and Voice Therapy. Englewood Cliffs, Prentice-Hall, Inc., 1971.
7. Bouhuys, A.: Lung Volumes and Breathing Patterns in Wind Instrument Players. J. Appl. Physiol., 19:5, pp. 967-975, 1964.
8. Bouhuys, A.: Physiology and Musical Instruments. Nature, vol. 221, pp. 1199-1204, 1969.
9. Bouhuys, A.: Pressure-Flow Events During Wind Instrument Playing. Annals New York Academy of Sciences, pp. 264-275.
10. Brunnstrom, Signi: Clinical Kinesiology, Ed. 2. Philadelphia, F.A. Davis Co., 1966.
11. Cheney, E.A.: Adaptation to Embouchure as a Function of Dentofacial Complex. Amer. J. Orthodontics. vol. 35, pp. 440-end. 1949.
12. Chusid, J.G.: Correlative Neuroanatomy and Functional Neurology, Ed. 15. Lange Medical Publications, 1973.
13. Colenbrander, A., and Spivey, B.: Classification of Visual Performance. American Academy Ophthalmology and Otolaryngology Committee on Terminology.
14. Daniels and Worthingham: Muscle Testing - Techniques of Manual Examination, Ed. 3. Philadelphia, W.B. Saunders Co., 1972.
15. Darley, F.L.: Diagnosis and Appraisal of Communication Disorders. Englewood Cliffs, Prentice-Hall, 1964.
16. Darley, F.L., Aronson, A., and Brown, J.: Motor Speech Disorders, Philadelphia, W.B. Saunders Co., 1975.
17. Denenholz, B.: Music as a Tool of Physical Medicine. Music Therapy, pp. 67-84, 1958.
18. Dictionary of Occupational Titles. Ed. 3, Supplement 2, p. A-1. Washington, D.C., U.S. Department of Labor, 1968.
19. Eysaguirre & Fidone: Physiology of Nervous System, Ed. 2, Chapter 7-8, pp. 71-111. Chicago, Medical Publications, Inc. 1975.
20. Farber, Shereen D.: Sensorimotor Evaluation and Treatment Procedures for Allied Health Personnel. Chapter V, pp. 69-77, Indiana University Foundation, 1974.
21. Guyton, A.C.: Organ Physiology: Structure and Function of the Nervous System. Chapter 7, pp. 95-107, W.B. Saunders Co., 1976.
22. Hayes, A.N.: Audiology. p. 216. New York, Appleton-Century Crofts, Inc., 1958.
23. Johnson, W., Darley, F., and Spriesterbach, D.: Diagnostic Methods in Speech Pathology. New York, Harper & Row, 1965.
24. Joint Motion: Method of Measuring and Recording. Chicago, American Academy of Orthopaedic Surgeons, 1965.
25. Kochevitsky, G.: The Art of Piano Playing. Evanston, Summy Birchard Co., 1967.
26. Lovius, B., and Huggins, D.G.: Orthodontics and the Wind Instrumentalist. J.Dent. Ed. 2, pp. 65-67, 1973.
27. Malick, M.H.: Manual on Dynamic Hand Splinting with Thermoplastic Materials. pp. 12-41. Pittsburgh, ABC Press, 1974.
28. Moyer, R.: A Handbook of Orthodontics. Chicago Yearbook, 1956.
29. Michel, D.E.: Music Therapy: An Approach to Therapy and Special Education Through Music. Springfield, Ill., Charles C. Thomas Publications, 1976.
30. Moore, P.: Organic Voice Disorders. Englewood Cliffs, Prentice-Hall, 1971.
31. Nordoff, P., and Robbins, C.: Music Therapy for Handicapped Children. Rudolf Steiner Publications, Inc., 1965.
32. Ortmann, O.: The Physiological Mechanics of Violin Technique. London, Paul. 1929.
33. Palmer J., and LaRusso, D.: Anatomy for Speech and Hearing. New York, Harper & Row, 1965.

34. Peinkoger, K., and Tannigel, F.: Handbook of Percussion Instruments. Schott, Belwin-Mills Publishing Corp., 1969 (English Translation, 1976.)

35. Perkins, W.: Speech Pathology: An Applied Behavioral Science. St. Louis, C.V. Mosby, 1971.

36. Porter, M.M.: Single Reed Instrument - Lip Shield. pp. 441-443. British Dental Journal, Nov. 1967.

37. Porter, M.M.: Single Reed - Restorative Dentistry. pp. 590-593. British Dental Journal, Dec. 1967.

38. Porter, M.M.: Brass Instruments. pp. 183-186. British Dental Journal, Feb. 1968.

39. Porter, M.M.: Brass Instruments. pp. 227-231. British Dental Journal, March 1968.

40. Porter, M.M.: Brass Instruments. pp. 271-274. British Dental Journal, March 1968.

41. Porter, M.M.: Brass Instruments. pp. 321-325. British Dental Journal, April 1968.

42. Salzman, J.A.: Principles of Orthodontics. p. 475. Philadelphia, Lippincott, 1950.

43. Spackman, W.: Occupational Therapy, Ed. 4. Philadelphia, J.B. Lippincott, 1963.

44. Strayer, E.R.: Musical Instruments as an Aid in the Treatment of Muscle Defects and Perversions. Vol. 9, pp. 18-27, Angle Orthodontist, 1939.

45. A Survey of Medicine and Medical Practice for the Rehabilitation Counselor. Washington, D.C., U.S. Department of Health, Education, and Welfare, 1966.

46. Tissler, H.: Particular Dental Care for Musicians. Vol. 49, pp. 48-49. Oral Hygiene, 1959.

47. Trombly, C., and Scott, A.D.: Occupational Therapy for Physical Dysfunction. Baltimore, The Williams & Wilkins Co., 1977.

48. Weast, R.D.: Brass Performance - An Analytical Text of the Physical Processes, Problems and Techniques of Brass. McGinnis & Marx, 1961.

49. Weast, R.: Brass Performance: An Analytical Text. New York, McGinnis and Marx, 1961.

50. Wells, Katherine: Kinesiology, and the Scientific Basis of Human Motion, Ed. 5. W.B. Saunders Co., 1971.

51. Yost, G.: Basic Principles of Violin Playing. Pittsburgh, Vokwein Brothers, Inc., 1940.

52. Zemlin, W.: Speech & Hearing Science. Englewood Cliffs, Prentice-Hall, 1968.

DATE DUE

SEP 2 5 2002	
JUN 0 9 2004	

BRODART   Cat. No. 23-221